CONTENTS

About the Authors

Randy Petersen is a free-lance writer living in Westville, New Jersey. Formerly the executive editor of *Evangelical Newsletter* and *The Bible Newsletter,* he has also worked with young people and written curriculum for youth and adults.

Eric Potter is a free-lance writer living in Fredericksburg, Virginia. He is a former editor for the David C. Cook Publishing Co. He has written for several David C. Cook series including *Hot Topics Youth Electives* and *Pathfinder Electives.*

Nelson E. Copeland, Jr. is a nationally known speaker and the author of several youth resources including *Great Games for City Kids* (Youth Specialties) and *A New Agenda for Urban Youth* (Winston-Derek). He is president of the Christian Education Coalition for African-American Leadership (CECAAL), an organization dedicated to reinforcing educational and cultural excellence among urban teenagers. He also serves as youth pastor at the First Baptist Church in Morton, Pennsylvania.

Ellen Larson is an educator and writer with degrees in education and theology. She has served as minister of Christian education in several churches, teaching teens and children, as well as their teachers. Her experience also includes teaching in public schools. She is the author of several books for Christian education teachers, and frequently leads training seminars for volunteer teachers. Ellen and her husband live in San Diego and are the parents of two daughters.

O.T. Speedway

Duffy Robbins

Randy Petersen

David C. Cook Publishing Co.
Elgin, Illinois—Weston, Ontario

Custom Curriculum
O.T. Speedway

Published by David C. Cook Publishing Co.
850 North Grove Ave., Elgin, IL 60120
Cable address: DCCOOK
Series creator: John Duckworth
Series editor: Randy Southern
Editor: Randy Southern
Option writers: Eric Potter, Nelson E. Copeland, Jr., and Ellen Larson
Designer: Bill Paetzold
Cover illustrator: Jack DesRocher
Inside illustrator: John Hayes
Printed in U.S.A.

ISBN: 0-7814-5000-4

You've Made the Right Choice!

Thanks for choosing **Custom Curriculum**! We think your choice says at least three things about you:

(1) You know your group pretty well, and want your program to fit that group like a glove;

(2) You like having options instead of being boxed in by some far-off curriculum editor;

(3) You have a small mole on your left forearm, exactly two inches above the elbow.

OK, so we were wrong about the mole. But if you like having choices that help you tailor meetings to fit your kids, **Custom Curriculum** *is* the best place to be.

Going through Customs

In this (and every) **Custom Curriculum** volume, you'll find
- five great sessions you can use anytime, in any order.
- reproducible student handouts, at least one per session.
- a truckload of options for adapting the sessions to your group (more about that in a minute).
- a helpful get-you-ready article by a youth expert.
- clip art for making posters, fliers, and other kinds of publicity to get kids to your meetings.

Each **Custom Curriculum** session has three to six steps. No matter how many steps a session has, it's designed to achieve these goals:

- *Getting together.* Using an icebreaker activity, you'll help kids be glad they came to the meeting.

- *Getting thirsty.* Why should kids care about your topic? Why should they care what the Bible has to say about it? You'll want to take a few minutes to earn their interest before you start pouring the "living water."

- *Getting the Word.* By exploring and discussing carefully-selected passages, you'll find out what God has to say.

- *Getting the point.* Here's where you'll help kids make the leap from principles to nitty-gritty situations they are likely to face.

- *Getting personal.* What should each group member do as a result of this session? You'll help each person find a specific "next-step" response that works for him or her.

Each session is written to last 45 to 60 minutes. But what if you have less time—or more? No problem! **Custom Curriculum** is all about ... options!

What Are My Options?

Every **Custom Curriculum** session gives you fourteen kinds of options:

• *Extra Action*—for groups that learn better when they're physically moving (instead of just reading, writing, and discussing).

• *Combined Junior High/High School*—to use when you're mixing age levels, and an activity or case study would be too "young" or "old" for part of the group.

• *Small Group*—for adapting activities that would be tough with groups of fewer than eight kids.

• *Large Group*—to alter steps for groups of more than twenty kids.

• *Urban*—for fitting sessions to urban facilities and multiethnic (especially African-American) concerns.

• *Heard It All Before*—for fresh approaches that get past the defenses of kids who are jaded by years in church.

• *Little Bible Background*—to use when most of your kids are strangers to the Bible, or haven't made a Christian commitment.

• *Mostly Guys*—to focus on guys' interests and to substitute activities they might be more enthused about.

• *Mostly Girls*—to address girls' concerns and to substitute activities they might prefer.

• *Extra Fun*—for longer, more "rowdy" youth meetings where the emphasis is on fun.

• *Short Meeting Time*—tips for condensing the session to 30 minutes or so.

• *Fellowship & Worship*—for building deeper relationships or enabling kids to praise God together.

• *Media*—to spice up meetings with video, music, or other popular media.

• *Sixth Grade*—appearing only in junior high/middle school volumes, this option helps you change steps that sixth graders might find hard to understand or relate to.

• *Extra Challenge*—appearing only in high school volumes, this option lets you crank up the voltage for kids who are ready for more Scripture or more demanding personal application.

Each kind of option is offered twice in each session. So in this book, you get *almost 150* ways to tweak the meetings to fit your group!

Customizing a Session

All right, you may be thinking. *With all of these options flying around, how do I put a session together? I don't have a lot of time, you know.*

We know! That's why we've made **Custom Curriculum** as easy to follow as possible. Let's take a look at how you might prepare an actual meeting. You can do that in four easy steps:

(1) *Read the basic session plan.* Start by choosing one or more of the goals listed at the beginning of the session. You have three to pick from: a goal that emphasizes *knowledge*, one that stresses *understanding*, and one that emphasizes *action*. Choose one or more, depending on what *you* want to accomplish. Then read the basic plan to see what will work for you and what might not.

(2) *Choose your options.* You don't *have* to use any options at all; the

basic session plan would work well for many groups, and you may want to stick with it if you have absolutely no time to consider options. But if you want a more perfect fit, check out your choices.

As you read the basic session plan, you'll see small symbols in the margin. Each symbol stands for a different kind of option. When you see a symbol, it means that kind of option is offered for that step. Turn to the page noted by the symbol and you'll see that option explained.

Let's say you have a small group, mostly guys who get bored if they don't keep moving. You'll want to keep an eye out for three kinds of options: Small Group, Mostly Guys, and Extra Action. As you read the basic session, you might spot symbols that tell you there are Small Group options for Step 1 and Step 3—maybe a different way to play a game so that you don't need big teams, and a way to cover several Bible passages when just a few kids are looking them up. Then you see symbols telling you that there are Mostly Guys options for Step 2 and Step 4—perhaps a substitute activity that doesn't require too much self-disclosure, and a case study guys will relate to. Finally you see symbols indicating Extra Action options for Step 2 and Step 3—maybe an active way to get kids' opinions instead of handing out a survey, and a way to act out some verses instead of just looking them up.

After reading the options, you might decide to use four of them. You base your choices on your personal tastes and the traits of your group that you think are most important right now. **Custom Curriculum** offers you more options than you'll need, so you can pick your current favorites and plug others into future meetings if you like.

(3) *Use the checklist.* Once you've picked your options, keep track of them with the simple checklist that appears at the end of each option section (just before the start of the next session plan). This little form gives you a place to write down the materials you'll need too—since they depend on the options you've chosen.

(4) *Get your stuff together.* Gather your materials; photocopy any Repro Resources (reproducible student sheets) you've decided to use. And . . . you're ready!

The Custom Curriculum Challenge

Your kids are fortunate to have you as their leader. You see them not as a bunch of generic teenagers, but as real, live, unique kids. You care whether you really connect with them. That's why you're willing to take a few extra minutes to tailor your meetings to fit.

It's a challenge to work with real, live kids, isn't it? We think you deserve a standing ovation for taking that challenge. And we pray that **Custom Curriculum** helps you shape sessions that shape lives for Jesus Christ and His kingdom.

—The Editors

Teaching the "Biblically-Impaired"
by Duffy Robbins

I was one of those kids who never knew much about the Bible. It wasn't that my parents didn't care enough to ever take me up to church; I think a big part of the problem was that the church never seemed to care enough to come down to me. Like most kids I squirmed, doodled, and daydreamed my way through Sunday sermons and Sunday school with little or no awareness of the wonderful, flammable, life-changing truths of the Scripture.

I counted the lights in the sanctuary. I scouted out who they might land on were they to fall down. My eyes trained on the woman four rows ahead, I practiced my mind control: "Mrs. Jones, pick your nose ... pick your nose ..."

It was never apparent that anyone seriously tried to engage the minds of kids like me. Maybe it was because they didn't feel there was much to work with. I don't know.

What I do know is that this week there will be Sunday school rooms and church pews filled with kids who are just like I was. They know little or nothing about the Bible. They think "John 3:16" is a bathroom somewhere on the third floor. When asked to find Israel, they look to a map of South America. When people start praising God in church, these kids are confused about why everyone is raising their hands and shouting "Honolulu!" ("Must be some town in South America. . . .")

Zip (???!!) through the Old Testament

I don't know about you, but when I think about doing a survey of the Old Testament with junior high kids, the word that comes to mind is not "zip"—"slip" maybe; possibly even "slit" (as in throats and wrists). But the word "zip" just seems a little naive. I mean, let's face it, for the average junior high kid, levitical sacrifice is not exactly a burning issue!

And yet, the Bible is an amazing book. In the pages of the Old Testament we can find every kind of human emotion, remarkable tales of victory, tragedy, romance, intrigue, hatred, and warmth. These pages have all the drama of an afternoon soap opera.

How to communicate these life-changing truths in such a way that we can ignite in junior highers a flame of interest in God's Word—that's the trick. It seems like everything is working against us. We're teaching students who often see the Bible as a musty, dusty old relic that doesn't speak to their modern lives. They are given in school ideas and information that seem to contradict the Bible. On top of that, some of us teach in a classroom setting that is less than perfect (too small, too big, too drab, too hot, too cold, too empty). And then, add to that a group of junior highers who have an MTV attention span, who got all of their early learning from a big yellow bird on television!

Cracking the "Zip" Code

It can be a little intimidating (a phrase similar to the one used by Custer just before he charged the Indians at Little Big Horn). But it isn't impossible. Here is a quick look at some of the difficulties you might face, and some practical suggestions that may help you crack the "zip" code.

Problem #1: Geography. The Old Testament is a book of names and places. It's like a trail guide in that the book makes a lot more sense if you have some idea of what the map looks like. Obviously, a map of the Holy Land will be a very useful teaching aid. But don't stop there.

Use slides or videos to help kids get a sense of what these places look like. Help them see that there really is a place called Jericho, and there really is a wall in Jerusalem. Remember, these are MTV kids. They are used to watching what they hear.

You might even find it helpful to make an impromptu map in your classroom, using signs to label certain kids as one country so that your students can see how Israel moved from one place to the next. I know one youth worker who actually had a huge map of the Holy Land painted on the church parking lot so she could literally walk her students from one country to the next. (The oil stain under the church bus was affectionately identfiied as Sodom and Gomorrah.)

Problem #2: Names. Unfortunately, the names in the Old Testament are not going to be familiar to the average teenager. Most of these names are about six syllables longer than any name they ever hear in school. And realistically, how many girls do you meet named Gomer (Hosea 1:3)?

Sometimes a little creativity can help make a name stick. Pharaoh is easy to remember because he was so "unfair-oh" to Israel. Saul, the first king of Israel, was a big man, tall, dark, and handsome, but once you've seen him on the outside you've seen it all—"S'all" there is to the guy. He had no heart.

Roleplays can also help kids identify names and actions. Labeled hats, robes, shields, badges, and sashes can make a conversation between little-known Bible characters a bit more concrete and memorable.

Use abbreviations when possible. Why call a mean king Nebuchadnezzar, when you just call him "Butch"? Let your students give the characters nicknames based on what they observe in the text.

Problem #3: Language. The language of the Old Testament is strange to our modern ears. We don't speak in psalms very often, and the only "prophecies" most people ever read are inside a fortune cookie. Teenagers can't learn what they can't understand, so we're going to have to make very certain that we bridge the language gap.

Without trying to offend anyone, I would strongly suggest that we can begin to accomplish this by simply making sure that our students are using a translation of the Bible that is comfortable for them. I'm sorry, but that probably means King James is out. You may want to use some of your budget to purchase some modern language translations of Scripture that will always be on hand every week in your classroom.

I've also found it helpful to photocopy the text we plan to study in a particular lesson. By doing this, I am getting a readable translation of the text into the hands of my students, and I am giving all of my group a common translation to read from. It must be pretty confusing for a thirteen year old when he hears someone reading aloud from a verse—the very same verse he is reading, but without any of the same words that he is seeing in his own Bible. The handout copy of the text can also serve as a worksheet so that kids will feel comfortable circling key words or underlining phrases.

Problem #4: Culture/history. The culture of the Old Testament is foreign to us. Kings, sacrifices, prophets, idols, satraps, parbars, ephods—the average junior higher can sometimes go weeks without using any of these terms. I strongly suggest that you gain access to a good Bible handbook as you work through this material. Sometimes understanding the story behind a custom, or the history behind an incident changes a passage from black and white to technicolor. Take time to set the stage and explain the setting so that students can really understand the action once the drama starts.

Problem #5: Too much stuff. One of the greatest dangers in a course like this is trying to cover everything in detail. One English puritan of the late 1600s preached on the Book of Job for eight years! While you've got to appreciate the guy for being thorough, you have to figure he wasn't drawing a large young teen crowd.

Remember that this series is designed as a survey course. That means your job is to give kids an overview. You'll want to be careful not to get bogged down by details ("OK kids, let's try it again until we get it right: 'The sons of Eliphaz the first-born of Esau: the chiefs Teman, Omar, Zepho, Kenaz ...'"). The purpose of this series is to give kids a sense of the flow of the Old Testament, not to trace every single tributary.

Don't allow yourself to be controlled by the material. Remember, the curriculum is a tool to serve you. It is better to cover only half of the lesson and have students learn, than cover everything but have the students remember nothing.

Zip or Zapped?

Our challenge in this series can be intimidating, but our opportunity is equally stunning. The very God whose power is so evident in the pages of the Old Testament wants desperately to speak to your students, and He will do so through you as you teach His Word. Remember that when you enter the classroom, you are accompanied by the living Lord. This is the same God who created the universe, parted the Red Sea, defeated the pagan prophets on Mount Carmel, and helped David slay Goliath. It may take a miracle, but He ought to be able to handle your junior high class!

Duffy Robbins is chairman of the Department of Youth Ministry at Eastern College in St. Davids, Pennsylvania. He is also a well-known conference speaker, seminar leader, and author.

The images on these two pages are designed to help you promote this course within your church and community. Feel free to photocopy anything here and adapt it to fit your publicity needs. The stuff on this page could be used as a flier that you send or hand out to kids—or as a bulletin insert. The stuff on the next page could be used to add visual interest to newsletters, calendars, bulletin boards, or other promotions. Be creative and have fun!

What Can You Learn from These People?

Plenty! Join us as we journey on the *O.T. Speedway*—a zip through the Old Testament! If you think the Old Testament is just a bunch of dusty, out-of-date stories, think again!

Who:

When:

Where:

Questions? Call:

O.T. Speedway

A Zip Through the Old Testament

Let's start at the beginning.

Have you heard the news?

EXTRA FUN

Take two tablets and call me in the morning.

See for yourself!

CUSTOM CURRICULUM

The World Gets Going

YOUR GOALS FOR THIS SESSION:

Choose one or more

☐ To help kids gain familiarity with the stories in the beginning of Genesis, developing a basic biblical literacy.

☐ To help kids understand how God has given choices to human beings from the start—we may choose to obey Him or not.

☐ To help kids recognize the choices involved when they are tempted—and choose to do right.

☐ Other _____
_____

Your Bible Base:

Genesis 1—11

Aliens: The Icebreaker

(Needed: Paper, pencils)

To open the session, set up the following situation: **Steven Spielberg is planning a new movie about an alien from another planet. But he's run out of ideas. Amazingly enough, he's asked our group to help him create this extraterrestrial being.**

Ask group members to begin thinking about some qualities they would give this alien. They should consider not only its external features, but also internal features such as emotions and intelligence.

Divide into teams of 3-5 people. Appoint a notetaker for each team, and give him or her paper and a pencil. Team members will pool their ideas to "create" an alien with as many details as they can think of. Their goal is to come up with something that Spielberg would be proud of.

After two or three minutes, bring all the teams together. Have each notetaker report on his or her team's creation. Note the differences in the details of the different aliens created.

A Choice Situation

(Needed: Copies of Repro Resource 1)

Ask volunteers to describe how they felt as they were "creating" the alien beings. Then ask: **How do you think God felt as He was creating the world? Do you think He had fun with it?** Try to get group members to compare their own feelings of creativity with the feelings they think God might have had. For instance, were they pleased with the final results of their creation? Do they think God was pleased with the final results of His creation? Did they create alien creatures that they'd like to know personally? Did God create creatures that He'd like to know personally?

After you get a few responses, try to shift your discussion to focus on the issue of *choice*. Ask: **Did you give your alien creatures the ability to choose freely?**

If your group members didn't consider the issue of choice while they were creating, have them think about the following questions: **Does your alien creature have the ability to do whatever it wants, whenever it wants? Or is your creature programmed like a robot to do certain things?**

After a few people respond, point out that God created human beings with the ability to choose freely, giving us the opportunity to decide between obedience or disobedience to Him.

Ask: **What difference does freedom of choice make? If you created an alien with free choice, how would it be different from an alien with no choice?** (Obviously, the alien with no choice would be like a robot. It would merely be an extension of its creator's will. Giving a creature free choice makes things interesting. The creature becomes more of a "person.")

To illustrate this point, ask for four volunteers to perform a brief skit. Give each volunteer a copy of "The Battle of the Mad Scientists" (Repro Resource 1). (Any of the characters in the skit can be male or female, depending on your volunteers.) Give the actors a minute to read through the script, then have them perform.

Afterward, ask: **What was the difference between the two scientists in the relationship they had with their humanoids? Who had the better relationship?** (Obviously, Alphonse had a fuller relationship with his creature, even though there was some hurt involved.)

Which of the scientists is most like God in His relationship with His creatures? Why? (Alphonse, because he gave his creature the choice to love him or not. He endured some sorrow, as God has, but he also has the joy of a creature freely loving him. It would not be as satisfying if he just "programmed" obedience and love.)

Summarize: **The whole history of the world goes back to this point: God gave humans the ability to choose. Sometimes we've chosen God's way, and He is pleased; sometimes we've chosen to disobey—and that hurts everyone. We see this played out very clearly in the early chapters of Genesis.**

Beginnings

(Needed: Copies of Repro Resource 2)

Divide into five teams, and assign each team the following Scripture passages. If your group is small, divide into pairs or assign passages to individuals.

    Team #1—Genesis 1:25-31; 2:15-17

    Team #2—Genesis 3:1-9, 22-24

    Team #3—Genesis 4:1-12

    Team #4—Genesis 6:9-14; 7:17-23; 8:18-21

    Team #5—Genesis 11:1-9

Distribute copies of "Scripture Search #1" (Repro Resource 2) and pencils. Members of each team, after reading and discussing their assigned passage(s), should fill out the sheet together.

After 10-15 minutes, gather the teams together, and have each one report its findings. Use the following information to supplement the teams' responses.

Team #1
Assigned Text: Genesis 1:25-31; 2:15-17
What title would you give this passage? ("Very Good," "Creation," "Where It All Began," etc.)

Who are the main characters? (God [the "us" may imply the Trinity]; His creation, including the first humans.)

What happened? (On the sixth day of creation, God decided to make human beings in His own image. As He looked on all His creation, He called it "very good.")

What choices (if any) were made? (God chose to make human beings. He also decided to prohibit them from eating from one particular tree.)

What were the consequences? (At this point, God's creation was wonderful. But God set Himself up for some pain with His one prohibition. He gave His creation the choice of whether to obey Him or not. In essence, He decided not to make robots.)

Team #2
Assigned Text: Genesis 3:1-9, 22-24
What title would you give this passage? ("Oops!" "The First Sin," "Watch What You Eat," etc.)

Who are the main characters? (Adam, Eve, the serpent, and God.)

What happened? (The serpent tempted Eve to eat the forbidden fruit. She convinced Adam to do so; and then they were ashamed to face God. They were cursed and thrown out of the Garden.)

What choices (if any) were made? (Adam and Eve chose to eat the fruit. God chose to punish them.)

What were the consequences? (Adam and Eve lost their intimate relationship with God. They were now subject to spiritual "death.")

Team #3

Assigned Text: Genesis 4:1-12

What title would you give this passage? ("The First Murder," "Cain Wasn't Abel," etc.)

Who are the main characters? (Cain, Abel, and God.)

What happened? (Abel presented a pleasing offering to God; Cain did not. In jealousy, Cain killed Abel and was punished.)

What choices (if any) were made? (Cain chose to give an offering that God would not like. [From verse 7, we can assume that Cain knew what was "right" to offer and chose not to offer it.] Cain chose to kill Abel.)

What were the consequences? (Cain was cursed, his livelihood as a farmer taken away, and he was forced to wander the earth.)

Team #4

Assigned Text: Genesis 6:9-14; 7:17-23; 8:18-21

What title would you give this passage? ("A Chance of Showers," "Noah Way," "The Flood," etc.)

Who are the main characters? (Noah and his family, the people of the earth, and God.)

What happened? (The people of earth were wicked, so God sent a flood to wipe them out. But he saved Noah and his family.)

What choices (if any) were made? (The people of the earth chose to displease God. Noah chose to obey God. God chose to punish the wicked.)

What were the consequences? (God sent a flood to kill the wicked. He allowed Noah to build an ark to save the righteous.)

Team #5

Assigned Text: Genesis 11:1-9

What title would you give this passage? ("The Tower of Babel," "Building Confusion," "Why We Have to Learn Foreign Languages," etc.)

Who are the main characters? (The builders of the tower and God.)

What happened? (Out of pride—and in defiance of God's command to fill the earth—the people began to build a tower that would "reach to heaven." God confused their languages so they could not work together in building it.)

What choices (if any) were made? (The tower builders chose to ignore God's command and build the tower.)

What were the consequences? (The builders' plans were thwarted and God scattered them.)

After all the teams have reported their findings, look back over all the choices that were made. Ask: **What pattern do you see in these choices and their consequences?** (Adam and Eve, Cain and Abel, Noah and his neighbors, the people of Babel—all had the opportunity to please God or not to. When they pleased and obeyed God, things went well. When they didn't, judgment came upon them.)

Ask: **Do these same choices and consequences still occur today? Have *you* ever experienced good consequences from obeying God or bad consequences from disobeying Him?** If volunteers feel like sharing their responses, let them. If not, just have group members consider the questions silently.

STEP 4

If I Had It to Do Over

(Needed: Copies of Repro Resource 3, chalkboard and chalk or newsprint and markers)

Ask for four volunteers to participate in a "reader's theatre" drama— one in which no stage movement or props are necessary. You'll need at least one guy and two girls. The fourth person (the "student" in the skit) may be either male or female. Distribute copies of "Second Thoughts" (Repro Resource 3) to your actors, and give them a minute to read through the skit. Then have them perform.

After the presentation, say something like: **It may seem that the choices of biblical characters are very different from the choices we face; but we can learn a lot from these characters. We too have serpent-like voices tempting us to partake of "forbidden fruit." And we often think we know more than God—or at least we act as if we do.**

Ask group members to list some of the temptations they face every day—at school, at home, with friends, etc. If they have trouble coming up with specifics, ask them what temptations they've faced in the past week. List group members' suggestions on the board as they are named.

After you've listed several items, ask: **If you gave in to some of these temptations, what do you think the consequences might be?** For instance, let's say one of the temptations on the list is

"cheating on a test at school." Possible consequences of giving in to this temptation might include failing the test (and perhaps even the whole course), getting a reputation as a "cheater," losing the respect of teachers and classmates, not learning important information, etc.

After group members have identified consequences for several of the temptations, ask: **How could you choose to please God in each of these situations?** In the case of cheating on a test at school, the obvious way to please God is to study extra hard for the test so that you lessen your need to cheat. Another less-obvious way to please God is to accept the consequences of not studying and be prepared to receive a legitimate "D" or "F" on the test.

Give group members time to respond to each situation listed. Then close in prayer, specifically asking God for strength in each of the tempting situations listed on the board.

The Battle of the Mad Scientists

VICTOR: So, Alphonse, what happened to the humanoid you created?

ALPHONSE: I told you before, Victor. It ran away.

VICTOR: I told you it was a mistake to give it a will of its own. Here, look at mine.
(*Calling*) Come here, 43B-7!

43B-7: (*Entering, robot-like*) You are the greatest mad scientist, Victor. You are the greatest.

VICTOR: See how happy it makes me?

ALPHONSE: That makes you happy? You programmed it to say that!

VICTOR: Yes, and didn't I do a great job?

43B-7: Yes, Victor, you did a great job. You are the greatest mad scientist.

ALPHONSE: Somehow, I just wanted more than a yes-man.

ADAM-12: (*Appearing in the doorway; he's a robot, but less robot-like than 43B-7*) A yes-humanoid, you mean.

ALPHONSE: Of course, Victor, that's want I meant.

VICTOR: I didn't say anything. It's your humanoid, Adam-12, back from its wanderings.

ADAM-12: I'm sorry I went away. I thought I could make it on my own. I was wrong. I need you.

ALPHONSE: Welcome back, Adam-12. It's good to see you.

ADAM-12: You mean you'll take me back? You're the
greatest, Alphonse.

43B-7: No, you're the greatest, Victor.

VICTOR: Thank you.

43B-7: (*Breaking down*) You're the greatest.
You're the greatest. Greatest.
Great— Gggrrrr.

ALPHONSE: I think 43B-7 is due
for a tune-up, Victor. Come on,
Adam-12, let's go shoot some hoops.

Scripture Search 1

After reading your assigned passages, answer the following questions as well as you can. You may have to do some extra thinking for some of the questions, because the answers may not be obvious in your text.

Assigned Text: _____

What title would you give this passage? _____

Who are the main characters? _____

_____

What happened? _____

_____

_____

_____

What choices (if any) were made? _____

_____

_____

What were the consequences? _____

_____

_____

Second Thoughts

CAIN: I wish I had it to do over again.

EVE: Tell me about it.

CAIN: Let me finish, Mom. I spent half my life crowing about how unfair God was. He had me wandering around the world. I would talk to anyone who would listen. "God plays favorites," I said. "You have to do it His way or not at all."

EVE: You got that right.

CAIN: I know. I finally heard what I was saying. "You have to do it His way." I knew the kind of offering He wanted, a blood offering, but I wanted to give Him some fruit.

EVE: It was fruit that got us into this mess.

CAIN: I know. I just thought I knew better. Why shouldn't God accept the fruit from my farm? He should! And I was going to make Him.

EVE: You wanted to be a god yourself.

CAIN: Yeah, and I played God by taking Abel's life. "Take that, God! If you won't let me make my offering, I won't let you enjoy Abel's!" And he was gone. I still hear his blood crying out.

EVE: And I still hear the rustle of the trees in Eden. The good trees, that is, which God gave us for food. But the serpent sounded so sincere. It seemed to make sense. How could I have been so stupid?

NOAH'S WIFE: I was stupid too. For a while.

CAIN: We all were.

NOAH'S WIFE: When God told my husband to build that ark, I thought it was the silliest thing. Rain? What was rain? Flood? Get real. I almost didn't go with him.

CAIN: You would have missed the boat.

NOAH'S WIFE: You could say that. But I'm glad Noah didn't listen to me. I know now that he was the only one listening to God. No one else cared about God in that world.

EVE: Listening to God. That's the key, isn't it? I let that serpent talk me into ignoring what God said.

CAIN: And I thought I had a better idea than God.

STUDENT: Hey, I'm kind of lost and I need some directions. You see, I'm a junior high student, and there are a lot of questions I'm facing right now. I was wondering if you could help me.

CAIN: Shoot.

EVE: Don't say that, son. It makes me nervous.

STUDENT: Well, my friends at school are into, like, partying and sex and drugs and all that. And I know the Bible says that you have to watch out for that, but it seems like it's not that much of a problem. I mean, these really aren't bad kids. And if they can handle it, maybe it's not so bad. What do you think?

EVE: Seems I've heard that story before. Be careful who you listen to.

CAIN: God's way really is best—even if you think it doesn't make sense at the time.

NOAH'S WIFE: Open your eyes, my friend. Those people are destroying themselves. But God will provide a way out for you.

EVE: Does that make any sense to you?

STUDENT: A little. But I'm not sure you guys really know what I'm going through. Thanks for trying, anyway.

CAIN: Can you believe that? He [she] is just going to repeat our same mistakes!

EVE: Careful! That's one of my children you're talking about. May God be with him [her]!

NOAH'S WIFE: Amen. Now let's get out of here. It's starting to rain.

Step 1

Try one of the following ways to liven up group members' creation of extraterrestrial beings. Instead of having teams write descriptions of the aliens, provide them with markers and posterboard; then have them draw posters of their aliens. Encourage them to depict the creature in such a way that they convey not only its appearance but also its inner qualities such as emotions and intelligence. After the teams have finished, have them explain their posters to each other. Another alternative would be to provide teams with aluminum foil or modeling clay and have them sculpt aliens, which they then can present to the rest of the group.

Step 3

Replace Repro Resource 2 with a guess-your-identity game. You will need tape and index cards with the names of the following Bible characters written on them: God, Adam, Eve, the serpent, Cain, Abel, Noah, his family, someone who didn't believe Noah, a builder of the Tower of Babel. Have group members form teams and assign each team one of the passages listed in the text. Instruct the teams to read their passages and then summarize them for the rest of the group. Then tape an index card to each person's back, making sure group members don't know who their character is. Have kids try to discover the identity of their characters by asking yes or no questions. Encourage them to ask questions which focus on choices their characters might have made and the consequences of those choices. For example, "Did I choose to give God an offering He didn't like?" or "Did God punish me for eating the forbidden fruit?" When everyone has discovered his or her character's identity, discuss the relationship between choices and consequences.

Step 2

Since you won't have much of an audience, downplay the performance aspect of the dramatic piece. Rather than having volunteers perform the "Battle of the Mad Scientists" skit, assign the parts and simply have your group members read them aloud.

Step 3

To ensure that kids can still work in groups of three or four people, divide them into two teams and assign one set of passages to each team. In choosing the passages, try to find one set that shows a good choice and one set that shows a bad choice. For example, the "Team #1" passages show a good choice (God's creation of the world) and the "Team #5" passages show a bad choice (building the Tower of Babel). You can summarize the other passages for your group members. Another alternative would be to assign passages to pairs and then summarize the unassigned passages.

Step 2

Actively involve more kids in the "Battle of the Mad Scientists" skit by dividing your group into smaller groups. Assign each group its own spot in the room. Then have four volunteers from each group perform the skit for the group. You may want to have group members stay in these smaller groups to discuss the skit, since it will make it easier for more of them to share their ideas. When you reconvene the entire group, have volunteers from each small group share their groups' findings.

Step 3

To encourage all of your group members to actively participate in the Bible study, make sure that teams have no more than five members. To do so, you may have to assign some teams the same passage. Smaller teams make it easier for shy group members to contribute. Another way to encourage participation by all is to have each team assign a specific duty to its members. For example, team members might designate a note taker, a leader to keep the discussion on task, a reader to read the passages, a reporter to share the team's findings with the rest of the group, etc. Another possibility is to have team members divide up the questions on the work sheet so that each member answers one question.

Step 3

Before turning to the Bible for examples of people making good and bad choices and living with the consequences, get kids' interest by discussing some current examples—real people whose choices profoundly affected their lives. Try the following examples or come up with some of your own.

• *Magic Johnson*—He chose sexual immorality and contracted AIDS, which will probably lead to his death. (Point out that AIDS is not a punishment for all sexual immorality, but that sin does have consequences.)

• *Milli Vanilli*—These guys chose to lip sync other people's music and pass it off as their own. When they got caught, their careers were destroyed.

• *Spike Lee*—He avoided the temptations of drugs, gangs, and dropping out of school. Instead, he chose education and now has a career as a filmmaker.

If possible, have group members come up with other examples. When you're finished discussing contemporary examples, look at examples of people from the Bible who faced similar temptations to be disobedient, dishonest, and foolish.

Step 4

Instead of doing the reader's theater piece, "Second Thoughts" (Repro Resource 3) divide group members into teams. Have the members of each team brainstorm a list of at least five temptations they face every day. Then have each team choose one of its temptations (such as cheating on a test), and write and perform a skit illustrating the temptation, a good or bad choice regarding that temptation, and the consequences of that choice. After each team performs its skit, discuss the temptation, ways of avoiding it, and ways of making the right choice.

Step 3

Your group members might find it helpful if you provide them with some background about Genesis before they look up the passages. You could explain, for example, that Genesis is the first book of the Bible and that its title means "beginning." Explain that, as the title indicates, the book deals with beginnings: how God created the world and some of the first things that happened.

Step 4

As you emphasize the importance of not giving in to temptations and of making God-pleasing choices, kids unfamiliar with the Bible might be wondering how a person knows what will please God or how to overcome temptation. Explain that the Bible teaches us principles about how God wants us to live. If we study it and learn those principles, then we will be able to examine each situation and decide which choice would please God.

You might also point out what should be our motivation in obeying. We shouldn't choose the right thing merely to avoid bad consequences (though we often do). Instead, we should choose the right thing because it will please God. For example, the reason for not cheating isn't that we might get caught, but that cheating would displease God.

Step 1

Begin the session with this pair-up-and-share game. Have group members form two lines of chairs, facing each other. (Make sure each line has the same number of chairs and people. If you have an odd number of kids, fill in the empty spot yourself.) Have group members pair up with the person across from them and complete the following statement: "One of the worst choices I've made is …" After group members have had a few minutes to share, instruct each person to move one chair to the right. (The two kids on the end will have to switch lines.) Then have group members pair up with their new partner and complete this sentence: "One of the best choices I've made is …" Afterward, you can either start the create-an-alien activity or go to the skit in Step 2, depending on your time .

Step 4

End the session with a short worship time, using directed prayer. Ask for a volunteer (or volunteers) to be prayer leader(s). If you have no volunteers, you could lead. The prayer time should emphasize the choices that God gives us. The leader will make a general statement, followed by time for silent prayer. The sequence might go something like this: "Dear God, thank you for giving us choices, especially allowing us to choose to love and obey you." (Silent prayer.) "We confess that we don't always make wise choices." (Silent prayer.) "Thank you for the times You helped us make wise choices." (Silent prayer.) "Help us make wise choices in the future." (Silent prayer.) "Amen."

Step 3

After teams have reported their findings, talk about the specific choices and consequences as they relate to your girls' immediate environment. Ask group members to consider whether they think girls' choices and/or consequences are different from guys' choices and consequences. Talk about the opportunities your group members have to choose to please God and the opportunities they have to choose to displease Him.

Step 4

Ask four girls to participate in the "reader's theater" drama by reading "Second Thoughts" (Repro Resource 3). Before they present the reading, ask them to adapt it slightly. Have the girl reading the part of Cain delete the words in response to Eve and read the rest of what Cain says as if she were reading from his diary. Ask the girl reading the part of Eve to talk as if she were reflecting on what Cain has written in the diary, rather than taking part in a dialogue with him. Change the ending so that the girl reading the part of Cain can tell the others that she knew Cain enough to speak for him, and she knew he'd probably say . . .

Step 3

After the teams have read their passages and completed the worksheet, have them review the material by playing "Genesis Baseball." Collect the worksheets from each team. Then combine teams so that you have two teams. Have Team A step up to the plate. Ask one of the questions off the sheets. If the first "batter" gets it right, the team gets a hit; if he gets it wrong, the team gets an out. After three outs, let Team B bat. Keep track of the runs that each team scores. When the game is finished and the kids have become familiar with all the passages, discuss the patterns of obedience and disobedience.

Step 4

Guys may not be comfortable with "reader's theater," especially if it calls for women's roles. So, instead of the "Second Thoughts" piece, have them make a list of the top five temptations that guys face. Begin by having each guy list the top five temptations that he thinks guys face. Instruct group members to consider the following categories: girls, school, girls, family, girls, sports, and girls. To encourage honesty, have them do the lists anonymously. Collect the lists. Then, with the help of a volunteer, list the temptations on a chalkboard or newsprint and keep a tally of how many times each one was mentioned. From this count, make the group's top five list. Discuss the list, especially the consequences of various choices, what the Bible says about the temptations, and ways to overcome them.

Step 1

Use the following game in place of the aliens icebreaker. Or, if you have a lot of time, use it before that icebreaker. Introduce the theme of the session by playing "Choice and Consequences." Go around the room asking group members questions. If a person answers a question correctly, give him or her a prize, such as a piece of candy. If he or she answers incorrectly, give him or her a consequence, such as singing the first line of "The Star-Spangled Banner" or doing five pushups. Make sure that you ask each person at least one question. You can make up questions, such as, "Who is the Secretary of State?" or get questions from Trivial Pursuit or a Bible trivia game. After the game, encourage group members to recognize that our choices have consequences. If we choose right, the consequences are good; if we don't, the consequences are bad.

Step 4

End the session with a back-to-Genesis costume party. You can do it one of two ways: either tell group members beforehand to come dressed as a character (or animal) from Genesis or have them make their own costumes at the end of the session. If you choose the latter, you'll need to provide scissors, tape, markers, and construction paper. To reinforce the idea of choices and consequences, you might make a rule that no one can have refreshments unless he or she has a costume.

Step 3

Instead of having teams fill out the worksheet for their passages, have them create news broadcasts. You will either need several video cameras, blank tapes, a television, and VCR; or you will need several tape recorders and blank audiocassettes. Encourage group members to be creative. For example, if they tape a television broadcast, they could have an anchorperson provide the background along with field reporters who interview key "eyewitnesses." For a radio broadcast, the format could be the same, using an announcer who introduces various special reports along with interviews. Encourage group members to use the worksheets as a guide in constructing their reports. In particular, you want them to focus on what people chose, what happened as a result, and why. Let them play their broadcasts for the rest of the group; then discuss patterns in the stories.

Step 4

Use the following idea to help group members list and explore the choices and and temptations that they face. Bring in scissors and a stack of old magazines. Youth-oriented magazines such as *Teen* and *Seventeen* are a good place to start. You might also look at special interest magazines on topics like cars, bodybuilding, skateboarding, music, etc. Have group members cut out pictures in which someone is faced with a choice. Discuss as many of the pictures as possible, using questions such as the following: **What choice is the person making (or facing)? What might be the consequences of this choice? What would be a better choice for this person?**

Step 1

Instead of working through Step 1, give a brief explanation of what freedom of choice means. Then ask: **If you were going to create a robot, would you give it freedom of choice? Why or why not? What difference does freedom of choice make? If you created a robot with free choice, how would it be different from a robot with no choice?** After discussing these questions for a few minutes, ask for volunteers to perform the "Battle of the Mad Scientists" skit in Step 2. Another possibility is to begin with the skit, using it as a way of discussing choice versus non-choice and the choice that God gave His creatures at creation. You could also save time by having volunteers read the skit rather than perform it.

Step 3

Rather than looking closely at all of the Bible passages, choose one or two to concentrate on. Make sure that the passage(s) you choose clearly shows the results of obedience and disobedience. For example, in the story of Cain and Abel (Team #3), Abel's obedience and sacrifice pleases God whereas Cain's doesn't. As your time allows, you can summarize what the other passages show about making choices and reaping consequences.

Step 1

To really get the creative juices going, give group members the name of the movie the alien will appear in. Allow them to determine whether it will be a good or bad alien. Some urban box office smashes could include:
• *The Homeboy from Outer Space*
• *The City Park Moon Dog*
• *Cosmic Dumpster Man*
• *The Big Thing on the 63rd Floor*
• *It Came from Saturn but Smelled Like Downtown*

Step 4

Before you begin the skit, have each teen make three columns on a piece of paper. Column #1 should be labeled, "Little Choices I Make Daily"; Column #2 should be labeled, "Big Choices I Make Just by Living in the City"; and Column #3 should say "Big Choices I Make That I'm Sure Are Not in the Bible." Give group members a few minutes to fill in their lists. Then ask volunteers to share some of their answers. This should serve as an effective lead-in to the skit and primer for the discussion afterward.

Step 2

Since many high schoolers would find the "Battle of the Mad Scientists" skit "beneath" them, expand your discussion of the advantages and disadvantages of freedom of choice. Discuss, for example, how freedom might affect personal relationships. Ask: **How would you like it if your best friend (or boyfriend/girlfriend) was programmed to like (love) you? What would be the advantages? The disadvantages?** Follow up this discussion by asking how freedom of choice affects our relationship with God.

Step 4

Take advantage of your high school students' experience and maturity by making them a panel of experts to address questions and problems from the rest of the group. Distribute pencils and slips of paper. Have your junior highers write questions about a situation or temptation. For example, "What's wrong with smoking pot a few times at a party?" or "Is it really that big a deal to use a crib sheet during a test?" When the junior highers are finished, collect their questions. Then, as moderator, pull out one of the questions, read it, and let the panel members respond. They may give biblical principles, share how they would handle it, or give examples from their own experience or that of friends. Allow the rest of the group members to ask follow-up questions if they want to. Go through as many questions as you can.

Step 3

Sections of "Scripture Search #1" (Repro Resource 2) may be difficult for some teams of sixth graders. To help kids feel more comfortable with this assignment, instruct the teams to choose three questions to answer on the sheet. Then, when the teams report back, work as a group on answering each team's unanswered questions.

Step 4

Help your sixth graders be more specific about temptations and consequences. Ask them to identify some of the "serpent-like voices" that influence and tempt them (commercials, peers, lyrics, feelings of inferiority, etc.). Talk about some actions that can be taken concerning the temptations. Ask: **Can some of your temptations be avoided? If not, how can you change the consequence by not giving in to the temptation?**

Date Used:

Approx.
Time

**Step 1: Aliens:
The Icebreaker** _____
o Extra Action
o Fellowship & Worship
o Extra Fun
o Short Meeting Time
o Urban
Things needed:

**Step 2: A Choice
Situation** _____
o Small Group
o Large Group
o Combined Junior High/High School
Things needed:

Step 3: Beginnings _____
o Extra Action
o Small Group
o Large Group
o Heard It All Before
o Little Bible Background
o Mostly Girls
o Mostly Guys
o Media
o Short Meeting Time
o Sixth Grade
Things needed:

**Step 4: If I Had It to
Do Over** _____
o Heard It All Before
o Little Bible Background
o Fellowship & Worship
o Mostly Girls
o Mostly Guys
o Extra Fun
o Media
o Urban
o Combined Junior High/High School
o Sixth Grade
Things needed:

How the Chosen People Got Chosen

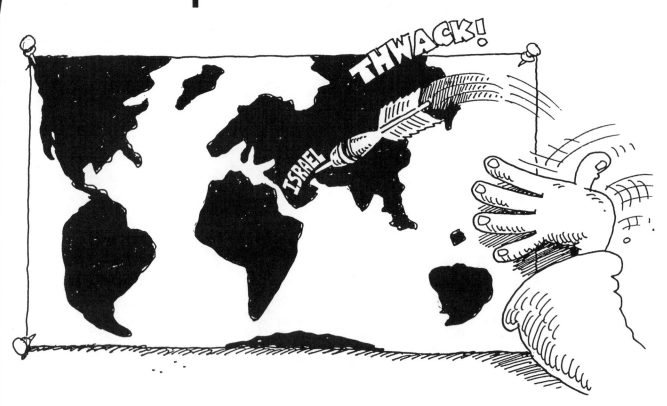

YOUR GOALS FOR THIS SESSION:

Choose one or more

☐ To help kids gain familiarity with the stories in Genesis and Exodus, developing a basic biblical literacy.

☐ To help kids understand that God makes promises to His people and keeps those promises.

☐ To help kids rely on God's promises in their daily attitudes and actions.

☐ Other _____
_____

Your Bible Base:

Genesis 12—Exodus 3

Party Time

Divide the group into three teams of equal size. Announce that each team is a political party and is in the midst of a presidential campaign. Instruct each team to hold its "convention" in one corner of the room.

At its convention, each team should: (1) come up with a name for its political party; (2) select a candidate to represent the party; and (3) come up with five campaign promises—things the candidate will do if he or she is elected to office.

Emphasize that everyone on the team should have an equal say in the convention. Don't let a few people monopolize the process. Explain that you'll be holding an "election" later in the session and that group members will be voting on the basis of the campaign promises.

Encourage group members to have fun with this activity; but also urge them to consider some serious questions too. What do citizens really want and need? What promises will they respond to? If you feel that national issues are too much for your group members to deal with, try a campaign for control of the town council—or even for the leadership of the group.

After about five minutes, bring the parties together. Explain that everyone has to vote for one of the *other* parties' candidates. No one may vote for his or her own party's candidate.

Have each candidate give a one-minute speech, listing his or her party's campaign promises. Then have group members vote by raising their hands. Give the winning candidate a "seat of honor" at the front of the room, next to you.

Lemon Pledge

Ask: **In our imaginary campaign, which promises "worked" and which didn't? Why?** (The promises that usually work are those that appeal to or would benefit the most people. The promises that probably wouldn't work are those that are too outrageous or those that obviously couldn't be kept.)

In real political campaigns, how do people decide who to vote for? What role do campaign promises play in people's decision-making process? (Many people vote for candidates not only only on the basis of what he or she promises, but on his or her ability—and dependability—to keep those promises.)

What if I were running for office, and I promised a high-paying career in the future for each of you if I were elected? Would you vote for me? Why or why not? Get a few responses.

What if I had a history of breaking campaign promises— saying that I would do certain things, and then not doing them? Would that affect your opinion of me? Would it change your mind about voting for me? Get a few responses. Ask group members to explain their responses.

Avoid getting involved in a political debate here. Steer away from discussion of specific candidates. That's not the point of this activity. The point is that we have to answer two major questions concerning cam-paign promises—or promises of any kind:

• Can the promiser be trusted to try to keep the promise?

• Is the promiser able to keep the promise?

Explain that today's session focuses on God as a promiser. He prom-ised many things to Abraham, Moses, and other Bible characters. And He promises things to us. Can He be trusted?

Fast Forward

(Needed: Copies of Repro Resource 4, copies of Repro Resource 5, pencils)

Give each kid in your group a copy of "All in the Family" (Repro Resource 4) and assign a reader for each part. If you have a small group, you may need to assign two or more roles to each reader. Explain that you're going to be covering a lot of history today. This reading will help your group members see the events through the eyes of the people involved. It will also help them get a broad idea of what was happening.

Give your readers a round of applause when they finish. If there are any questions about the material, try to postpone them. They may be answered in the following activity.

Divide into four teams, and assign each team the following Scripture passages. If your group is small, divide into pairs or assign passages to individuals.

Team #1—Genesis 12:1-4; 15:5, 6; 17:1-8
Team #2—Genesis 25:27-34; 28:10-15
Team #3—Genesis 37:23-28; 39:1-6; 45:3-8
Team #4—Exodus 3:1-10

Distribute copies of "Scripture Search #2" (Repro Resource 5) and pencils. Members of each team, after reading and discussing their assigned passage(s), should fill out the sheet together.

After 10-15 minutes, gather the teams together, and have each one report its findings. Use the following information to supplement the teams' responses.

Team #1
Assigned Text: Genesis 12:1-4; 15:5, 6; 17:1-8
What title would you give this passage? ("Bless You," "Starry-eyed," "The Covenant," etc.)
Who are the main characters? (Abram [Abraham] and God.)
What happened? (God promised to give Abram many descendants and a land to live in. He wanted Abram to move to that land.)
What did God promise? (Descendants and land.)
What were the "terms" of this promise? (Abraham needed to trust the promise, to obey God, and to make the move to the new land.)

Team #2
Assigned Text: Genesis 25:27-34; 28:10-15
What title would you give this passage? ("A Birthright for Stew: The Deal of the Century," "Strange Dreams," "Stairway to Heaven," etc.)
Who are the main characters? (Jacob, Esau, and God.)
What happened? (Jacob tricked Esau out of his birthright [Esau's inheritance rights for being firstborn]. Later God renewed His promises to Jacob.)
What did God promise? (Countless descendants for Jacob, land, and blessing to all people through Jacob.)
What were the "terms" of this promise? (None, really. In fact, it's amazing that Jacob, known for his trickery, would receive such a blessing.)

Team #3
Assigned Text: Genesis 37:23-28; 39:1-6; 45:3-8
What title would you give this passage? ("The Brothers and the Cistern," "All Things Work Together," "Oh, Brother!" etc.)
Who are the main characters? (Joseph and his brothers.)
What happened? (Joseph was sold into slavery in Egypt by his brothers. In Egypt, Joseph rose to fame and power, and was eventually reunited and reconciled with his brothers.)
What did God promise? (No explicit promise is given; but God was with Joseph, and helped him prosper and succeed in everything he did.)
What were the "terms" of this promise? (There are no explicit "terms" given; but Joseph was obedient and faithful to God.)

Team #4
Assigned Text: Exodus 3:1-10
What title would you give this passage? ("The Burning Bush," "Let My People Go," "When Shrubbery Talks, Listen," etc.)
Who are the main characters? (Moses and God.)
What happened? (God told Moses to confront Pharaoh, and demand the release of Israelite slaves.)
What did God promise? (Awareness of His people's suffering and rescue from slavery in Egypt.)
What were the "terms" of this promise? (Moses had to lead the Israelites out of Egypt.)

Can I Buy a Vow?

(Needed: Copies of Repro Resource 5, pencils)

Ask: **Does God still make promises to us today like He did to people in Bible times?** (Though He may not appear personally to us like He did to people in Bible times, God does indeed still make promises to us today.)

Where can we find the promises God gives us? (The Bible)

What are some of the promises He gives us? Use the following suggestions to supplement group members' responses:

• He will be with us always (Matthew 28:20).
• He will give believers eternal life (John 3:16).
• He will forgive us for our sins upon confession (I John 1:9).
• He will answer those who call upon Him (Jeremiah 33:3).
• He will supply the needs of believers who sacrifice for Him (Philippians 4:19).
• He will never forsake His own (Hebrews 13:5).

What do we have to do to receive these promises? (All we really have to do is to *claim* them, to trust in them, to rely on them.)

Summarize: **The amazing thing in the stories we read is that Abraham, Jacob, Joseph, and Moses really didn't have to do much. Their "contract" with God was rather one-sided. Yes, it took guts for Abram to move to a new, unknown land—but if God was telling the truth, it was a great new opportunity for him. He believed God, and he acted on that belief.**

It's like someone saying, "Here's a mansion in Beverly Hills. It's yours, free. All you have to do is move there." Who's saying it? If it's a friend who's as broke as you are, forget it! But if it's Ed McMahon from the Publisher's Clearinghouse Sweepstakes, start packing!

God has promised you all this great stuff—forgiveness, eternal life, and so on. It's just like a campaign promise—you have to decide (1) whether He means what He says, and (2) whether He's able to do it. If you decide that you believe His promises, then you just have to act on that belief.

He's saying, "Here's a way of life that's better than anything you've ever known." But you won't really have that life until you try it out.

Ask group members to think of one of God's promises that they

need to believe, claim, and act on. Give them a few minutes to think.
Ask them to write the promise on the back of Repro Resource 5. Then
have them write down one specific thing they can do to act on this
promise. For instance, if someone wanted to claim God's promise of
forgiveness, he or she would act on that promise by praying to Him the
next time he or she did something wrong.

Close the session in prayer, thanking God for His great promises.

ALL IN THE FAMILY

ABRAHAM: I guess it started with me, Abraham. God promised to give me many descendants—a great nation, He said—and a land we could all live in. All I had to do was leave my homeland.

SARAH: That was tough to do. I'm Sarah, Abraham's wife. But I think the hardest thing to believe was that God would give us a son. I was already in my 80's and we had no children. Talk about your biological clock!

ISAAC: But then I was born, miraculously. I'm Isaac, the "child of promise." I was precious to Abraham and Sarah. But then one day, God told Dad to take me up to a mountain and perform a sacrifice.

ABRAHAM: Isaac was going to be the sacrifice, though he didn't know it. What could I do? God had been faithful to me. I had to be faithful to Him. I figured that God could raise Isaac from the dead if He wanted.

ISAAC: Fortunately it didn't get that far. There I was, strapped to the altar. Dad had the knife in his hand, but God's angel stopped him. I was saved. But I've been a bit wary of camping trips ever since.

REBEKAH: I'm Rebekah. Isaac married me, and we had two sons, Jacob and Esau. Jacob was my favorite, but Ike liked Esau. It was a pretty good deal—Esau hunted for food and Jacob cooked it. But they didn't get along very well.

JACOB: You see, Esau was a few minutes older than I was, so he was in line to get all of God's promises. But he didn't care about God's promises. He just liked to eat and hunt.

ESAU: So one day Jacob tricked me. I came home hungry for Jacob's homemade stew, and he wouldn't give me any unless I gave him my rights as the oldest son. So I did.

ISAAC: And then Rebekah and Jacob both tricked me into giving Jacob my fatherly blessing. I was going blind, and Jacob dressed up like Esau—so I blessed the wrong kid!

JACOB: Anyway, Esau was pretty ticked, so I had to skip town. I went to Haran, where we had relatives. I got a job with my uncle Laban, who had two daughters—the beautiful and talented Rachel, and her older sister Leah.

LEAH: Jacob promised to work seven years to win Rachel's hand in marriage. But Daddy thought it was uncool for the younger one to get married first. So there was a wedding after seven years but—surprise!—it was me, Leah, under the veil.

RACHEL: So Jacob worked another seven years to marry me. Daddy and Jake were always tricking each other. It was a mess. So one day Jacob and I moved out—oh, and Leah came too.

JACOB: We went back to Canaan, the land of Abraham and Isaac. God had promised my grandfather a great nation of descendants, and we got a good start on it. In all, my wives had twelve sons. But my favorite was Joseph, the son of my beloved Rachel.

JOSEPH: That's me. And OK, maybe I was a bit uppity, but my brothers picked on me. They finally sold me as a slave to some traders heading for Egypt. In Egypt, I had all sorts of adventures. First, I became the chief slave in my household, but the master's wife falsely accused me of rape. So I went to prison, where I became sort of the assistant to the jailkeeper.

PHARAOH: That's when I had a dream. I'm Pharaoh, ruler of Egypt. Only Joseph could interpret my dream. He said God was telling us to prepare for famine. So I put him in charge of the whole project. He was second-in-command in Egypt.

JOSEPH: And this was great—my brothers got so hungry during the famine that they had to come to Egypt to get food. They had to come to me, except they didn't know it was me. Eventually I told them who I was and invited them all to move to Egypt and live with me.

MOSES: Hundreds of years passed. Joseph and his brothers had children, who had children, and so on. It was quite a large bunch now. But there were new rulers in Egypt who had forgotten all about Joseph. They enslaved the descendants of Jacob—who were now called Israelites. That's where I came in. I'm Moses, raised as an Egyptian but really an Israelite. God spoke to me one day, ordering me to go to the Pharaoh and say, "Let My people go!" I was kind of shy about it, but I did it. And the rest, as they say, is history.

Scripture Search ②

After reading your assigned passages, answer the following questions as well as you can. You may have to do some extra thinking for some of the questions, because the answers may not be obvious in your text.

Assigned Text: _____

What title would you give this passage? _____

Who are the main characters? _____

What happened? _____

What did God promise? _____

What were the "terms" of this promise? Did the people involved have to do anything to receive it? _____

Step 1

Use one or more of the following suggestions to make the campaign activity even more active. Provide markers and poster board so kids can make posters for their candidates. Encourage the kids to cheer, clap, and chant for their candidates. When they vote, instead of a show of hands, decide who wins according to whoever gets the most applause.

Step 3

Rather than filling out Repro Resource 5, have the teams play Bible Pictionary. After the teams read their passages, have each team make up three cards—one with a character name, one with the promise, and one with the terms of the promise. Collect the cards, shuffle them, and make a stack. Have teams join together so that you have two teams. Have a volunteer from Team A pick up a card and draw on a chalkboard or newsprint the clue on the card. The team that correctly guesses the clue on the card first gets a point. Then have someone from Team B take a card and draw. When the game is finished, review as a group the promises and terms in each passage.

Step 1

Instead of doing political campaigns, have group members write campaign promises anonymously and vote on which promises they find most believable. Distribute pencils and two slips of paper to each group member. When group members have written their promises, collect the slips of paper in a hat or paper bag. Then read aloud each promise and have kids indicate whether they find it believable by raising their hands, standing up, or shouting "I believe it." Keep track of the "yes" votes to determine which are the three most believable promises. (You might also want to keep track of the three least believable promises.) Follow up the activity by discussing what criteria group members used to decide if a promise was believable or not.

Step 3

Rather than having individuals or pairs work on the passages, choose a couple of the passages to work on as a group. You might choose the passages for Team #1 (God's promises to Abraham) and Team #4 (God's promise to rescue the Israelites from Egypt), since these passages offer a fairly clear promise with "terms" that the recipients of the promise had to follow.

Step 1

Keep kids actively involved in the campaigning by running primaries before the election. Divide your group into Democrats and Republicans. Further divide each party into three groups. These groups should choose a candidate and campaign strategies (as outlined in the main session). Then have each party run a primary to choose its candidate. Have candidates make their speeches, and let party members vote on their favorite. When each party has chosen its candidate, have those candidates give their speeches for the whole group. Then have kids vote on the candidates. (Make sure that the Democrats don't all vote Democrat, and vice versa, or you'll have a tie.) Follow up the election with a discussion of what makes campaign promises believable.

Step 3

Turn the "All in the Family" skit into a full-fledged performance. You will need eleven volunteers (seven guys and four girls). Give the volunteers copies of the skit before the session. Ask them to bring costumes. You might suggest the standard bathrobes for the men, along with some specifics such as a paper crown for Pharaoh, a bow and arrow for Esau, a big stick for Moses, and so on. Have the volunteers memorize their lines. Let them perform for the group—on a stage, if one is available. When the volunteers are finished performing, give them a big round of applause.

Step 3

Sometimes churched kids get turned off by the Bible because they've spent so much time reading passages and answering questions. As an alternative to Repro Resource 5, try one of the following ways to get group members to explore the assigned passages. Provide each team with markers and poster board. After reading their passages, have the teams either imagine the passage as a movie and make a poster to advertise it or have them make a mural depicting the events of their passage. Encourage them to pay attention to (and try to convey) what the passage shows about promises. Give the teams a few minutes to work. When they're finished, have them show their art work to the other teams. Give the teams time to ask questions and explain their work; then discuss God's character as promise-giver.

Step 4

Point out that, like Bible people, we can be comforted by God's promises. Using roleplay situations, have group members look at problems we face and how Bible promises could help us. As a group, brainstorm several problems that your group members face. Make a list of the problems on the board. (Among the problems group members might mention are loneliness, fear of the future, shyness, concern over appearance, feelings of unpopularity, fear of failure, and pressure regarding academics or athletics.) If you think your group members will be too shy to share honestly before the group, you could distribute index cards and have them write the problems. Then you could collect the index cards in a paper bag.
Then divide into teams and have each team pick one or two cards from the bag. The team members should roleplay scenes in which someone is struggling with the problem(s) on the card and other people are offering advice and comfort based on God's promises in the Bible.

Step 3

Instead of dividing into teams and assigning each team a passage, pick just a few of the passages to read and discuss as a group. You will probably want to give some background for the passages you pick. For example, if you picked the Team #2 passages about Jacob and Esau, you might want to explain that they were descended from Abraham, the father of the Jewish people. You might also explain the inheritance customs of that culture: the firstborn male was entitled to inherit twice as much of the father's wealth (land, animals, servants, etc.). Be sure to ask kids about any words or concepts that they find confusing. Finally, you may need to point out the verses in which the promise occurs. For example, in the Jacob and Esau passage, the promise comes in Genesis 28:13-15. If you have time after discussing these passages as a group, you may want to summarize the other passages. Or, you could recommend that the kids study them on their own sometime.

Step 4

If your group members are unfamiliar with the Bible, they won't be able to rattle off a list of God's promises. They need two things: to learn God's promises and to learn how to discover those promises on their own. To help them in this process, bring in some concordances. Explain that when you look up a word, the concordance shows which verses in the Bible that word occurs in. Instruct group members to look up *promise* and *promises* in the concordance; then have them look up some of the passages listed. Then explain that they can use the concordance to find out what the Bible says about things like salvation, eternal life, God's love, peace, patience, etc.

Step 1

Begin the session with the following icebreaker to help kids get to know each other better and to get them thinking about promises. Have group members form a single line, running from the tallest to the shortest. Pair them off according to height: the tallest and shortest together, the next tallest and next shortest, and so on. Instruct the pairs to complete this thought: "A promise that someone made to me and kept was …" They should also explain how the kept promise made them feel. Then, after a few minutes, have them complete this thought: "A promise that someone made to me and broke was …" They should also explain how the broken promise made them feel. When they're finished, you can either move on to the campaign activity; or, if you're short of time, discuss as a group what makes promises believable, focusing especially on what is promised and the character of the promiser.

Step 4

Conclude the session with a worship time that focuses on God's promises to us. After brainstorming promises found in the Bible, have group members look up the passages in which the promises are found. (You might supply concordances to help them do this.) Then have group members organize the passages into categories, such as promises about salvation, God's love, God's help, the resurrection, etc. Finally, have them choose at least one song that addresses God's promises or our response to them (e.g., "Trust and Obey," "Leaning on Jesus," "What a Friend We Have in Jesus"). Begin the worship time with prayer, thanking God for His many promises and for being trustworthy. Then have group members read passages of promise. After each promise is read, have the group members respond, "Lord, I believe, help my unbelief." You may want to include songs or prayers throughout. But sing at least one song to end the worship time.

Step 3
After the four teams report their findings from "Scripture Search #2" (Repro Resource 5), review the "All in the Family" skit that was read earlier. Ask your group members to put themselves into the lives of each of the women involved. Ask: **Were the problems and the "terms" of the promises any different for the women than for the men? Why or why not?**

Step 4
Use a chalkboard or newsprint to make a list of God's promises as your group members name them. If possible, include a few Bible verses that will further explain each promise. Have group members write down the list and verses on the back of Repro Resource 5. Ask them to identify on the list at least one promise that they have believed and have acted on in the past, and then to choose at least one promise that they need to believe, claim, and act on right now in their lives.

Step 1
Let the guys burn off some energy by parading their candidates on their shoulders during the campaign. You might also have the group carry the winning candidate on a victory march.

Step 3
The "All in the Family" skit probably won't go over real well with guys, especially since it has a lot of female roles. Skip the skit and spend some time on the following Bible study relay. You will need a large chalkboard and chalk or posterboard and markers for each team. After the teams have completed Repro Resource 5, have them share their answers through a relay. When you give the signal, the first person from each team should run to the board, do five jumping jacks, write the answer to the first question, and run back to his team. Then the second guy should run to the board, do five pushups, write the second answer, and return to the team. This should continue until all five answers have been written on the board. (Other exercises you might use for this activity include sit-ups, squat thrusts, and jumping in place.) The first team finished wins. Afterward, have teams read each other's answers and ask any questions they may have.

Step 2
You can use this idea in addition to or in place of the discussion of the campaign promises. Get group members thinking about what makes claims or promises believable by playing a doubting game. Have group members form a circle. Go around the circle and have each person say three things about himself or herself. (It could be something the person has done, something he or she likes, a personal characteristic, a hope for the future, etc.) Two of the statements should be true, the other false. The person to the speaker's right has to decide which is the false statement. If he or she guesses correctly, the speaker is out; if he or she guesses incorrectly, he or she is out. Play until there's only one person left and then declare that person the winner. Afterward, discuss the game using the following questions: **What made you believe or disbelieve each speaker? What makes us believe what people say?** Then explain that today's session focuses on God as a promise-maker and on the promises He makes.

Step 4
After group members come up with a list of biblical promises, divide them into teams. Instruct each team to choose a promise, and then rewrite the promise in the form of a rap song. Suggest that the raps include a situation that kids face in which the promise might be especially applicable. Here's an example for the promise that God will always be with us: "If you're feelin' down / And you don't know what to do / Just remember God / 'Cause He's always with you. / Huh huh huh huh." Give the teams a few minutes to work; then have them perform their raps for each other.

Step 1

Try one of these media-oriented variations for the campaign. Rather than having the candidates make speeches, have each "party" make up commercials for its candidate. The parties could create TV commercials, radio commercials, or both. You will need tape recorders and/or video cameras, blank tapes, and perhaps a VCR and TV. Limit the commercials to one minute (or two thirty-second spots). Encourage group members to emphasize campaign promises in their commercials. If you have time, you could provide them with poster board and markers and let them make posters or bumper stickers for their candidates. When everyone is finished, have the parties display their campaign paraphernalia and play their commercials. Wrap up the activity by having group members vote for their favorite candidate. (However, they must vote for someone other than the person from their own party.)

Step 2

A good way to explore what makes promises believable is to analyze promises made in commercials. You could do this in one of several ways. You might videotape some commercials before the session and then play them back for your group members. Or you might bring in a TV and watch some commercials during the session. Or you might bring in some magazines and have group members discuss the ads. In analyzing the commercials, have group members answer these questions: **What is the promise being made? Do you believe it? Why or why not? What role do promises play in advertising?** Pay special attention to comments regarding the credibility of the company or the person endorsing a product. Help group members see that believability has a lot to do with the character of the promise-maker. Use this insight to introduce a discussion of God's character and promises.

Step 1

If you're short of time, skip the campaign activity entirely. Go directly to Step 2. Begin the session by discussing how people choose which candidate to vote for in a real campaign. Your main emphasis in this opening discussion should be to get group members thinking about what makes a promise believable. Ask: **What criteria do you think a person should take into account when he or she is judging the believability of a promise?**

Step 3

Skip the "All in the Family" skit (Repro Resource 4) and move directly into studying the assigned passages. However, rather than having teams read and fill out worksheets, have them read or skim their passages and then appoint someone to summarize the passage for the other teams. Encourage group members to focus on the promises that God makes and the terms or conditions of those promises (if there are any). After the summaries are given, discuss God's promises and character, using the following questions: **Are God's promises believable? Why or why not?** (Yes. He has the power to keep them; His nature makes Him faithful to His word; the Bible shows God keeping His promises to His people.) **What does God expect of us when He makes promises?** (He expects us to believe Him and to obey whatever terms He sets.)

Step 2

In your discussion of the campaign activity, ask: **What if I were running for office, and I promised that there would be prosperity for everyone in the future—if we're willing to face some hard financial times for the next couple of years? Would you vote for me? Why or why not?** You may find that a lot of your group members would be willing to vote for you. Usually teens who have faced hard times in the past are willing to sacrifice so that others can be given financial security. On the other hand, those who have not wanted for much in life will often choose not to sacrifice that which will change their lifestyle, even if it is for a limited time.

Step 4

As you begin this step, don't assume that Christian and non-Christian teens from the city believe God does not speak today as in the Bible. Many urban young people will say they have had mystical experiences that they attribute to God. Ask: **How many of you believe that God talks to us today like He did to people in Bible times?** Of those who respond in the affirmative, ask if they will share any experiences they may have had. Be careful not to make judgments on your group members' experiences. Some may come from holiness or charismatic backgrounds for which this type of experience is valid and frequent. Instead, use this activity to demonstrate that God is still active on behalf of those who trust in Him, and that He is able to keep His promises.

Step 1

Your high school students will probably be more familiar with political campaigns, speeches, and promises than your junior highers will. Therefore, enlist your high schoolers as campaign managers. They should direct group discussions, keep their people on task, decide how to choose the candidate, and so forth.

Step 4

As you discuss the promises that your group members want to claim, the situations and experiences of your junior high and high school students are different enough to merit separate treatment. Divide your high school students and junior high students into two groups. Instruct the members of each group to discuss the problems they face in areas like dating, school, parents, siblings, and struggles with faith. Then have them discuss which of God's promises fit the problems they identified.

Step 1

If your sixth graders haven't had much experience with elections and campaigns, the opening activity may not work well with them. Instead, have them work as one team in coming up with a list of five things they think would improve their school and/or church. Then ask for five volunteers to give one-minute speeches to explain and support each of the items on the list. Afterward, have the group vote for the most convincing speech. Give that speaker a "seat of honor" at the front of the room.

Step 3

Sections of "Scripture Search #2" (Repro Resource 5) may be difficult for some sixth graders. To help your group members feel more comfortable with this assignment, ask the teams to choose three questions to answer as they work on their own. Then, when the teams report back, work as a group in answering the two unanswered questions from each team.

Date Used:

Approx.
Time

Step 1: Party Time _____
o Extra Action
o Small Group
o Large Group
o Fellowship & Worship
o Mostly Guys
o Media
o Short Meeting Time
o Combined Junior High/High School
o Sixth Grade
Things needed:

Step 2: Lemon Pledge _____
o Extra Fun
o Media
o Urban
Things needed:

Step 3: Fast Forward _____
o Extra Action
o Small Group
o Large Group
o Heard It All Before
o Little Bible Background
o Mostly Girls
o Mostly Guys
o Short Meeting Time
o Sixth Grade
Things needed:

Step 4: Can I Buy a Vow? _____
o Heard It All Before
o Little Bible Background
o Fellowship & Worship
o Mostly Girls
o Extra Fun
o Urban
o Combined Junior High/High School
Things needed:

SESSION

3 Seeing Things God's Way

YOUR GOALS FOR THIS SESSION:

Choose one or more

☐ To help kids gain familiarity with the Old Testament, from Moses to David, developing a basic biblical literacy.

☐ To help kids understand how adopting God's perspective can change their lives for the better.

☐ To help kids choose to live according to God's commandments and not just their own desires.

☐ Other _____
_____

Your Bible Base:

Exodus 20
Numbers 13—14
Joshua 24
Judges 7
1 Samuel 24

You're All Wet

(Needed: Blindfold, paper cup, pitcher of water, raincoat, large sheet of plastic, towels)

Ask for two volunteers to participate in a stunt. One will be seated and draped with a raincoat or something waterproof. This person will hold a paper cup on top of his or her head. The other person will be blindfolded and given a pitcher of water. [NOTE: Because this stunt involves water, you'll need to make sure that you've properly protected your floor or carpet with a large sheet of plastic before you try it.]

The object of the stunt is for the blindfolded person to pour the water into the cup. The seated person must give directions. The blindfolded person may not touch the cup or the seated person as he or she pours the water.

Most likely, the blindfolded person will miss the cup and will pour water all over the seated person. After a few tries, give the participants a round of applause—and some towels.

Then ask: **Why was it so hard to do this simple task? Pouring water into a cup—anyone can do that. What made it so difficult?** (The person doing the pouring was blindfolded; the person doing the directing couldn't really see what was going on.)

What if we'd had a third person involved, someone who wasn't blindfolded, standing next to the person doing the pouring, giving him (or **her**) **directions? Would that have made the task any easier? Why?** (Probably. The person would have had the perspective to guide the person doing the pouring.)

Explain that you're going to read a statement. Those who agree with the statement should stand as straight and rigid as possible. Those who disagree with the statement should slouch down in their seats. Those who aren't sure should stand slouched over.

Here's the statement: **To be successful in life, you have to be aware of how things really are.** Don't try to further explain or clarify the statement; have group members respond to it just as you read it.

After group members have responded, ask a few of them to explain their responses. Then point out that the statement is true. It was illustrated in the opening stunt. The blindfolded person may have had an *idea* about where the cup was; and the seated person may have had an *idea* about where the pitcher was. But for the stunt to be truly successful, they both would have had to know how things really were.

Explain: **Throughout the Old Testament, people got into trouble because they had false ideas about the way things were. God regularly revealed Himself to them, and He showed them how to live. But often people seemed to prefer their *own* views of how to live—even though they couldn't see how things *really* were. It's almost like they were living life behind a blindfold. They refused to see things God's way.**

STEP 2

Asking for Directions

(Needed: Copies of Repro Resource 6)

Ask for two volunteers to perform a brief skit. Give them each a copy of "Moses Supposes" (Repro Resource 6). Let them read through the script once; then have them perform.

Afterward, ask: **In between all the bad jokes, what did this skit say about God's law?** (It's like an instruction manual. It gives us directions on how to live.)

Do you know people who are like that VCR—blinking 12:00, 12:00, 12:00? They have great potential, but they're just not operating properly. Do you know anyone like that? Have group members silently consider their answers.

Do *you* ever feel like you need an instruction manual—some kind of directions for living your life? If so, when? Encourage volunteers to respond, but don't *force* anyone to share.

Moses received God's law—His "instruction manual"—directly from God Himself. Where can *we* find God's instructions for our lives today? (The Bible.)

[NOTE: Some of your group members may have negative attitudes toward God's law. They may think of His law as a list of dos and don'ts designed to spoil their fun. But God's law has a very practical aspect to it. He knows better than anyone else what is truly best for our lives. His law is a gift to us, to help us understand Him and to help us understand ourselves.]

OPTIONS

HEARD IT ALL BEFORE

MOSTLY GIRLS

MEDIA

SHORT MEETING TIME

URBAN

Word Perfect

(Needed: Copies of Repro Resource 7, pencils)

Explain: **We're going to look at the time immediately after Moses got the law at Mount Sinai. Then we'll trace some of the ups and downs of Israel's relationship with God.**

Divide into four teams, and assign each team the following Scripture passages. If your group is small, divide into pairs or assign passages to individuals.

Team #1—Numbers 13:17-20, 26-33; 14:1-9

Team #2—Joshua 24:14-24

Team #3—Judges 7:1-8, 16-21

Team #4—I Samuel 24:1-12

Distribute copies of "Scripture Search #3" (Repro Resource 7) and pencils. Members of each team, after reading and discussing their assigned passage(s), should fill out the sheet together.

After 10-15 minutes, gather the teams together, and have each one report its findings. Use the following information to supplement the teams' responses.

Team #1
Assigned Text: Numbers 13:17-20, 26-33; 14:1-9
What title would you give this passage? ("Grasshoppers," "Spy vs. Spy," "Paralyzed by Fear," etc.)
Who are the main characters? (Moses, Joshua, Caleb, and the other spies.)
What happened? (Twelve spies were sent into Canaan [the promised land] to scout it out. They reported that it was a beautiful, fertile land, but it would be difficult to conquer. Two spies, Joshua and Caleb, urged the people to move ahead in faith, but the people sided with the fearful spies.)
How would you describe the viewpoint of the people involved? (Joshua and Caleb viewed the situation through the eyes of faith. The other spies were blinded by fear.)
How would this compare with God's viewpoint? (God wanted to give the land to His people. He knew that He could win the victory for them. Joshua and Caleb were on the right track.)
Point out that the result of the people's decision not to enter Canaan was forty years of wandering in the wilderness. God would not let His

faithless people enter the promised land. Only Joshua and Caleb sur-
vived and participated in the conquest of Canaan forty years later.

Have group members silently consider the following: **In Numbers
13:33, the fearful spies say, "We seemed like grasshoppers *in
our own eyes*"** (emphasis added) **compared to the inhabitants of
Canaan. How often do we limit ourselves by a low view of
our own God-given abilities?**

Team #2
Assigned Text: Joshua 24:14-24
What title would you give this passage? ("Joshua's Last Stand," "Gotta
Serve Somebody," "I'm Not Joshin'!" etc.)
Who are the main characters? (Joshua and the people of Israel.)
What happened? (Joshua, shortly before his death, challenged the
people to serve God wholeheartedly. They voiced their commitment.)
How would you describe the viewpoint of the people involved? (Joshua
saw the importance of commitment to God. God had already worked
powerfully for Israel, and He would continue to do so, as long as the
Israelites relied on Him. The people apparently agreed.)
How would this compare with God's viewpoint? (This was exactly the
kind of commitment God wanted. It's a shame it didn't last long.)

Point out that Joshua adds a bit of reverse psychology in verses 19
and 20. He warns the people that serving God is difficult sometimes. If
they went back on their commitment, God would bring disaster. This
was exactly what happened in later times. "He will not forgive" (vs. 19)
has nothing to do with our forgiveness in Christ. It merely means that
God would not treat the people's rebellion lightly. It would have serious
consequences.

Say: **Verse 15 says, "If serving the Lord seems undesirable
to you, then choose . . . whom you will serve." Some people
today see Christianity as a kind of slavery. But the fact is that
everyone serves something. Some people are slaves to
money; some are slaves to sex; some are slaves to themselves. If we take an honest look around, we won't find a
more desirable master than God.**

Team #3
Assigned Text: Judges 7:1-8, 16-21
What title would you give this passage? ("Gideon's Smash Hit," "Small Is
Beautiful," "Salvation Army," etc.)
Who are the main characters? (God, Gideon, Gideon's army, and the
Midianites.)
What happened? (God called Gideon to lead an army against the
Midianites. Surprisingly, God thought Gideon's army was too large, and
whittled it down to a band of 300. Using trumpets, and torches hidden
inside clay pots, Gideon's army surprised the Midianites and scared them
away.)

How would you describe the viewpoint of the people involved? (Some of the original soldiers were afraid to go into battle, so God excused them. God was concerned that the Israelites would claim the victory for themselves—unless it was obvious that God was working a miracle. Apparently God was not a part of the Israelite's everyday thinking.)

How would this compare with God's viewpoint? (God wanted to show the Israelites how important He was in their lives.)

Point out that verse 2 says, "In order that Israel may not boast against me that her own strength has saved her..." The Israelites often forgot about God during the good times, thinking that they had achieved their own good fortune. Often we do the same.

Say: **The period of the Judges was a like a rollercoaster ride. God provided some great victories, like this one. But there was a lot of spiritual confusion. For long stretches of time, the Israelites would ignore God's law and behave like their Canaanite neighbors, even worshiping false gods. Gideon himself built an idol for people to worship in the aftermath of this great victory. The last few chapters of Judges are intense and shocking, full of the worst sex and violence. It's summed up in Judges 21:25—"In those days Israel had no king; everyone did as he saw fit."**

Team #4
Assigned Text: I Samuel 24:1-12
What title would you give this passage? ("On the Run," "Incident in a Cave," "The Lord's Anointed," etc.)

Who are the main characters? (Saul, David, and David's men.)

What happened? (Saul was pursuing David, jealous of David's popularity. While hiding out in a cave, David noticed that Saul came into the cave "to relieve himself." It would have been a perfect opportunity to kill Saul and become king. But David refused. Saul was still king, and deserved David's loyalty. David cut off a piece of Saul's robe, which he later showed to Saul to prove how harmless he was.)

How would you describe the viewpoint of the people involved? (David trusted that God would deal with Saul in his own way. Saul was blinded by jealousy, and sought to protect his throne through violence.)

How would this compare with God's viewpoint? (God was protecting David. He appreciated David's trust.)

Point out that David appeals to Saul in verse 10 to see "with your own eyes." Saul was closing his eyes to the truth about David. Only David seemed to see that God was the ultimate King—and both Saul and David would have to answer to Him.

Say: **David showed his faith by *not* acting in a situation where he could have advanced himself. Sometimes God wants us to wait for Him. But remember the Israelite spies in Numbers 13. They were *afraid* to act in a way God had** ordered them to act. Sometimes, when we see a situation God's way, we *must* act.

Saul or David?

(Needed: Chalkboard and chalk or newsprint and marker, copies of Repro Resource 8, pencils)

Ask: **In I Samuel 24, what did Saul seem to be concerned about? How did he see his situation?** (He was very self-centered, seeking to protect his own power, allowing his jealousy to control him.)

What was David concerned about? How did he see his situation? (He wanted to please God, to "do the right thing." He saw that God was ultimately in control—he just needed to be faithful and God would work things out.)

What was the "secret of success" we talked about earlier in the session? (To be successful in life, you have to be aware of how things really are.)

How was this shown in the lives of Saul and David? (David succeeded; Saul did not. Saul died an angry, bitter man, because he did not see that God wanted to work in his life. David became a great king, because he saw himself as a subject of a greater King.)

Let's talk about our lives. What situations do we face that require a certain "insight" to succeed? List group members' responses on the board. Supplement those responses with the following scenarios.

(1) Everyone has plans for Saturday night except you.

Ask: **What would the "Saul approach" to this situation be?** (Get desperate. Start to worry that everybody will laugh at you. Quickly try to find *anyone* to do something with—even if that person is all wrong for you.)

What would the "David approach" to this situation be? (Keep cool. Trust that God will provide someone if He wants to. Recognize that you may have to take some chances by approaching others, if that's what God wants. Determine not to lower your friendship/dating standards just to have something to do.)

(2) You promised your kid sister that you'd take her shopping; but then you got invited to a cool party.

Ask: **What would the "Saul approach" to this situation be?**

(Forget the kid; do the party. It's best for your own social advancement. The kid will still be there later.)

What would the "David approach" to this situation be? (Maintain your loyalties. Maybe the kid sister will reschedule; but if not, you have to keep your promise. In the long run, that's far more important.)

(3) A kid at school hurt you—badly. Now you want to get back at that person.

Ask: **What would the "Saul approach" to this situation be?** (Get revenge. Figure out something that will really hurt the person. People have to learn that they can't pull that stuff on you.)

What would the "David approach" to this situation be? (Forgive. Allow God to work. The person will either reap the consequences of his or her own actions, or perhaps will come to a point of repentance [through your gentle spirit].)

Hand out copies of "Vision Prayer" (Repro Resource 8). Explain: **I don't know what situations you're facing in your lives. But I know that, to deal with them properly, first you need to see them clearly. That's what our whole Bible study was telling us. As long as people saw God in control, and their own responsibility to Him, things were fine. But when they saw only the physical details of their situation, it was a disaster.**

Here's a sheet for you to start on now, but you should take it home with you and look at it throughout the week. Once you fill it in, it's a prayer you could pray each day.

First, tell God about some difficult situation you find yourself in. Whatever is weighing on you most right now, write that down. Give group members a minute or two to do so.

Then think about how you tend to look at this situation. What are your priorities, your fears, your desires, your expectations? Write those down too. Give group members a minute or two to do so.

Then ask God to tell you how He sees it. Stop and listen. Let God bring to your mind Scripture passages you've read. Think about any godly advice you've received. Let God talk to you about priorities and expectations.

That's something you may need to do at home, when you have some time to sit quietly before God in prayer. But write those things down as they come to you. Then, with God's guidance, you'll be able to figure out what to do about the situation.

Close the session in prayer, asking God to speak to each group member about the situation he or she wrote down.

Mōses Suppōses

REPORTER: We're here with Moses, leader of the Israelites. Recently, Moses led his people out of slavery in Egypt. But then you had some difficulties, didn't you, Moses?

MOSES: That's right. There was a major body of water in front of us, and of course we'd forgotten to pack our waterskis. But God worked a miracle and parted the water for us. Good thing, too, because the king of Egypt sent his army after us.

REPORTER: Why was that?

MOSES: He changed his mind about letting all of his slaves go free.

REPORTER: What did you tell him?

MOSES: He was all wet.

REPORTER: So you were headed for the Promised Land, the land of Canaan, where Joseph and his brothers used to live before they went down to Egypt.

MOSES: Right. But we had to stop at Mount Sinai to get directions.

REPORTER: Directions? Isn't it just "head northeast until you see the milk and honey"?

MOSES: No. I mean, we needed directions for our lives. God needed to tell us how He wanted us to live. I mean, we had no clue. People were worshiping anything that moved. "Oh, look, a lizard, worship it!" There was partying, fights, people getting drunk—it was like spring break every night of the week. So I went up the mountain and I told God what a headache these people were. And you know what He said?

REPORTER: Take two tablets and call me in the morning.

MOSES: You've heard that one before.

REPORTER: No, it's right here in the script.

MOSES: Right, well, anyway, He gave me His law. And I shared it with the people, and it was great. It was like—well, it was like this: One of our people invented a VCR the other day. This guy is brilliant. He invented a video cassette recorder, but we can't use it because no one has invented an instruction manual yet. So this thing is blinking 12:00, 12:00, 12:00 all across the desert. It's annoying. But that's what we're like without God's law—kind of blinking with no purpose. But God's law tells us how to operate. It's great!

REPORTER: Thank you, Moses. Now back to you, Homer, for an update on the massive relief efforts and clean-up going on in Egypt after the plagues.

Scripture Search ❸

After reading your assigned passage(s) and introduction, answer the following questions as well as you can. You may have to do some extra thinking for some of the questions, because the answers may not be obvious in your text.

Team #1 Introduction
After receiving the law at Mount Sinai, the Israelites continued to travel toward Canaan, the Promised Land. They stopped and sent a scouting party to check out the land.

Team #2 Introduction
After the Israelites wandered in the desert for 40 years, Joshua finally led them into Canaan. They won many great victories, conquering most of the land. At the end of his career, Joshua gathered the people and challenged them.

Team #3 Introduction
After Joshua, Israel entered an up-and-down period. Armies would invade, and some leader would arise to lead Israel's defense. In Judges 7, the Midianites are the strong army occupying Israel's land.

Team #4 Introduction
Israel finally got a king—Saul. But he turned out to be moody and sometimes crazy. So the prophet Samuel anointed a new king, David. Only he had to wait until Saul died. King Saul became jealous of the popular David and was trying to kill him.

Assigned Text: _____

What title would you give this passage? _____

Who are the main characters? _____

What happened? _____

How would you describe the viewpoint of the people involved? How were they seeing things? _____

How would this compare with God's viewpoint? _____

VISION PRAYER

Lord, here's my situation:

_____
_____
_____
_____

I am seeing it like this:

• My priorities are ...

_____
_____

• My fears are ...

_____
_____

• My desires are ...

_____
_____

• My expectations are ...

_____
_____

You see it like this:

_____
_____
_____
_____

This is what I need to do:

_____
_____

Step 3
Rather than having teams complete Repro Resource 7, have them creatively present their assigned passages to the rest of the group. One team might choose to have one person read the passage aloud while other group members act out what's being described. Another team might choose to draw a comic strip, portraying the events described in its passage. Another team might choose to put on a puppet show (using team members' socks for puppets) to communicate the events in its passage. Encourage the teams to be creative in their presentations. Have them focus on the idea of perspective—the perspective of the characters involved, as well as God's perspective.

Step 4
Rather than merely discussing the scenarios, have group members roleplay them. Assign two teams to each of the three scenarios. One team should come up with a "Saul approach" to the problem and the other team should come up with a "David approach." For example, in the situation in which everybody else has plans for Saturday night, the "Saul approach" team might portray a kid desperately calling people on the phone, begging and threatening them to do something with him or her. The "David approach" team might portray a kid writing his or her feelings in a diary (while speaking the words aloud). After each approach has been presented, ask: **What would be some other poor ways of handling this situation? What would be some other good ways of handling it?**

Step 3
Rather than dividing into teams, take advantage of your group's smallness and work through the passages together. Rather than having teams complete Repro Resource 7 individually, list the answers and principles on the board. If time doesn't permit you to discuss all the passages together, you may want to summarize some of them for the group. Be sure, though, to have group members read and discuss the passages about Saul and David (Team #4) since they will need them for Step 4.

Step 4
Your group's small size also gives you the advantage of closeness—or the opportunity to develop it. Such closeness can provide opportunities for fellowship and caring. After group members have filled out the "Vision Prayer" sheets (Repro Resource 8), have them share their situations with each other. If group members seem uncomfortable don't force them to share; but encourage as many volunteers as you can. You might encourage them by filling out the sheet yourself and being the first one to share. When all that want to have shared, spend some time praying for each other. You could assign who will pray for whom or you could have a time of sentence prayers.

Step 1
Rather than having most of your group members watch while one person soaks another, get them all involved in the following game. Have group members pair off. Give each pair a blindfold. The blindfolded partner should walk around the room while the other partner gives directions. The non-blindfolded partner must use only verbal directions and may not lead the other person by the hand. After a few minutes, have the partners switch roles. After both partners have had a turn being blindfolded, discuss as a group why the blindfolded person needed someone to give directions. Encourage group members to see that they needed someone who could see, someone who had a good perspective.

Step 4
Give more group members an opportunity to talk by breaking into small groups to discuss the Saul and David approaches. You can either instruct the groups to discuss all three situations, or you can assign one situation to each group and have that group come up with a skit or roleplay to illustrate the different approaches. Then, after each roleplay is presented, you could have the other groups brainstorm additional ways to handle such situations in a God-pleasing manner.

Step 2

Sometimes when people need help, Christians offer standard answers rather than real concern. Some of your group members may have heard "standard advice" so often that it no longer seems true. Allow these group members to express their feelings about easy answers and standard advice, but also help them see that the advice is true. To do so, replace the "Moses Supposes" skit with a discussion of typical Christian advice. Before the session, get seven or eight people to record pieces of advice and encouragement that Christians typically give to people facing problems (e.g., "Don't worry, just pray" or "God will take care of it," etc.) Play these statements to your group members. Then ask: **Is this advice comforting? Why or why not? Is it true? Why or why not?** Point out that although the phrases seem trite, they express the truth. Then turn to the Bible passages in Step 3 for examples.

Step 3

If your group members think that discussing differing viewpoints or perspectives on life has little to do with the problems they face, share the following sobering thoughts. Between 1970 and 1986, the suicide rate for high school students nearly doubled. Point out that many kids who kill themselves do so because they think there are no solutions to the problems they face. Many adults recognize that, while these problems are difficult and painful, they do have solutions. Adults realize this truth because they've lived through similar problems; their age and experience gives them a different perspective. If these young people could view their problems through an adult's eyes, they might determine to find solutions rather than killing themselves. If differing perspectives between people can make that much difference, imagine how much difference looking at things from *God's* perspective could make.

Step 3

You can help the teams better understand their passages by providing them with some background information. Here are some suggestions to get you started. Team #1: After God helped Moses and the Israelites escape from the Egyptians, He led them to Canaan, the land He had promised to give them. Team #2: After the people wandered in the wilderness for forty years and after Moses died, Joshua became the leader of the Israelites. With God's help, he led the people in conquering Canaan, which began with the battle of Jericho. In this passage, Joshua is old and near death, but he offers the people one last challenge. Team #3: During the time of Judges, the Israelites didn't have a king. Instead, when the people got into trouble, God raised up a judge to turn the people back to God and lead them out of danger, often by defeating their foreign oppressors. Gideon is one of those judges. Team #4: Eventually the Israelites got tired of judges and wanted a king like the other countries. So God anointed Saul. But, when Saul disobeyed God, God took the kingdom away from him and promised it to a new king—David—and his descendants. Consequently, Saul was trying to kill David, his political rival.

Step 4

Kids who haven't had a lot of Bible training may wonder what these stories about ancient people have to do with them. Reinforce the idea that the Bible gives positive and negative examples of faith and obedience. From these examples, we can learn principles that we can apply to our own lives.

Step 1

Depending on how much time you have, you can use this activity before the water-pouring activity or in place of it. Have group members form teams of four. Give each team a puzzle, made from a piece of construction paper, cut into seven or eight odd-shaped pieces. (You can make these ahead of time or give paper and scissors to the teams and let them make the puzzles.) Have the teams mix up the pieces of the puzzle, blindfold themselves, and try to put the puzzle together blindfolded. When they've finished, have them remove their blindfolds, mix up the pieces again, and put the puzzle together without the blindfolds. Afterward, discuss why it was easier to do the puzzle without the blindfolds, emphasizing the importance of seeing things clearly, of seeing the big picture.

Step 4

After group members have completed the "Vision Prayer" sheet (Repro Resource 8), use it as a guide for a group prayer time. If your group is large or the kids are uncomfortable praying about personal matters, use the categories on the sheet as cues for silent prayer. For example, the prayer leader could say, "Lord, here's my situation," and then give silent time for group members to pray about their situations. If your group members are comfortable about praying for personal matters (voluntarily, of course), use the categories on the sheet as cues for individual prayers. For example, the prayer leader could say, "I am seeing it like this: My priorities are ..." and then group members could pray what their priorities are. After going through the sheet, the leader should close the prayer.

MOSTLY GIRLS

Step 2
Add Moses' sister Miriam to the skit "Moses Supposes" (Repro Resource 6). Ask a volunteer to ad lib the part of an older sister who enjoys teasing her little brother. If some background is needed for Miriam's personality, read Exodus 2:4-8; 15:20, 21 and Numbers 12:1-15.

Step 3
Your group members may be interested in reading about a woman prophetess, who was a part of the period of Judges described for Team #3. You may want to add a Team #5 or use this in place of Team #3. The assigned text is Judges 4. Point out that Deborah followed God's laws as she led Israel. After the events described in Judges 4, the land had peace for forty years.

MOSTLY GUYS

Step 1
As an alternative to the water-pouring activity, play blindfolded dodgeball. Set up for a regular game of dodgeball. Divide group members into two teams. Have Team A split onto two sides of the room with Team B in the middle. The Team A players should throw the balls across the room, trying to hit one of the Team B players. But here's the catch: The Team A players have to wear blindfolds. Play for about five minutes. Award a point to Team A any time a Team B player gets hit (if that happens). Then have teams switch positions and play for five minutes. If you have time, let the teams play a few minutes each way without blindfolds. Discuss whether throwing or dodging was easier for the players. Emphasize the importance of perspective, being able to see what's going on.

Step 4
Use the following situations as supplements or alternatives in discussing the David/Saul approaches.
• **Situation A—You're playing a pickup game of basketball. A guy on the other team keeps fouling you but won't call the fouls himself or listen when you call them.** (Saul approach: Foul the guy back; hit him; quit playing. David approach: try to ignore him even though it's unfair; try to outplay him; avoid cheating.)
• **Situation B—You just got cut from the baseball team.** (Saul appraoch: Swear and get depressed; quit baseball; get mad at the people who made the team. David approach: Accept it; keep practicing; be glad for the people who made the team.)
• **Situation C—You have a crush on a girl, but aren't ready to tell her. Then some of your friends tell her friends about it.** (Saul approach: Deny the rumors; stop speaking to your "friends." David approach: Stay calm; be honest with the girl.)

EXTRA FUN

Step 1
As an alternative to the opening activity, have group members negotiate an obstacle course—blindfolded. Have group members form two teams. Instruct the members of Team A to leave the room and put on blindfolds. Have members of Team B set up chairs at random around the room in an obstacle course fashion. Bring in the members of Team A and have them try to negotiate the obstacle course. Then have the teams switch positions. Send Team B out of the room and have Team A rearrange the chairs. Then have Team B try to negotiate the obstacle course. You may want to award prizes—for "Most Creative Obstacle Course Technique," "Most Painful Fall," "Best Sportsmanship," etc.—to the contestants. Afterward, discuss how much easier the activity would have been if the contestants had had someone—someone who could see the course—giving them instructions as they negotiated the course.

Step 3
Instead of having teams complete "Scripture Search #3" (Repro Resource 7), have them prepare to play "Team Jeopardy." Instruct each team to read its assigned passage and write five answers (the clues) along with their accompanying questions (answers), based on the passage. (A sample clue might be, "They gave differing opinions about the land of Canaan." The accompanying question would be, "Who are the twelve spies?") The teams should write each answer and question on a slip of paper. Collect the slips in a paper bag. One member from each team will compete in each round. Read the clue (answer). If someone knows the question, he or she should shout "buzz." The first one to shout "buzz" gets to give the answer (it must be in the form of a question). Award a point to the team whose player answers correctly. Afterward, discuss as a group how the viewpoints of the people in the passages compared with God's.

Step 2
Instead of the "Moses Supposes" skit, have group members analyze the viewpoints expressed in some contemporary songs. Play one or more songs that express a viewpoint that is contrary to or at odds with God's viewpoint. If you can't think of any contemporary examples, try an older song like one of these: "It's My Life" by The Animals; "The Greatest Love of All" by Whitney Houston; or "Authority Song" by John Cougar Mellencamp. Use questions like these to discuss the song: **What viewpoint does it express? How does this viewpoint compare to God's? What do you think might be the consequences of holding such a viewpoint?**

Step 4
Bring in a stack of newspapers. Have group members form teams of three or four. Give each team a supply of newspapers. Instruct the teams to look for articles in which people faced some kind of problem. Have the teams decide whether the people in the articles faced the problem with a "David" or a "Saul" approach. As each team shares its article and conclusions with the rest of the group, discuss how a person faced with that problem might gain God's perspective and how that perspective might help the person solve the problem.

Step 1
Replace the water-pouring activity with the following brief drawing game. Have someone volunteer to be an "artist." Send this person out of the room. Explain to the rest of the group that you're going to give the artist directions for drawing a turtle. Bring the volunteer back and have him or her draw a figure on the board according to your instructions.
Give these directions:
(1) Draw a half circle.
(2) Draw a straight line to close off the half circle.
(3) Draw a small circle near it.
(4) Connect the half circle to the little circle with two lines.
(5) Draw five short lines on the half circle.
When the person is finished, ask what he or she drew. Does it look like a turtle? Discuss the perspective. Ask: **What difference would it have made if our artist had known what he (she) was drawing?**

Step 2
Skip the "Moses Supposes" skit (Repro Resource 6). Instead, point out that God's law is like an "instruction manual" for people. Then begin discussing the passages in Step 3.

Step 2
Before delving into this activity, be sure your teens know what it means to have potential. In many instances, urban teens view failure and achieving below their potential as being the fault of other people. For instance, you might ask, "Why did you fail the class, Johnny?" Johnny might respond, "Because the teacher didn't like me." Or you might ask, "Gina, what did you do to get locked up last night?" Gina might reply, "Nothing. The police just don't like girls who drink." While it's true that there is individual and systematic abuse that sidelines urban teens, these young people must own up to their probelms.
Help your group members consider that the source of their potential in God can be turned "on" only by accepting their whole selves. One way to do this is to have them fold a piece of paper in half. On one side, they should list good things about themselves; on the other, they should list bad things. Ask a few volunteers to share some of the bad things on their lists. Then ask them to explain why those bad things are prevalent. If someone tries to blame the traits on somebody or something else, point out that this is no excuse for not achieving one's potential. Consider reading the following Scripture passages: Philippians 4:13; Isaiah 40:28-31; II Corinthians 12:9, 10.

Step 3
For an extra spark, add to Repro Resource 7 this question: **What event(s) in our city is (are) similar to the events in this passage?** By doing this, you will assist teens in viewing Scripture in light of their present reality.

Step 3
In making up the teams for the Bible study, try to distribute the high school students evenly. High schoolers generally have more highly developed analytical skills than junior highers. These skills will be especially helpful in answering the fifth question on the worksheet: "How would this compare with God's viewpoint?"

Step 4
Junior high and high school students face different problems and different pressures. To help make this activity more applicable to high school students, you might want to add the following situations for them to discuss.
• **Situation A—You get a grade that you think is unfair.**
• **Situation B—You want to be invited to a certain party, but you know that you won't, since only the most popular people will be invited.**
• **Situation C—You didn't get accepted by your first-choice college.**

Step 3
Sections of "Scripture Search #3" (Repro Resource 7) may be difficult for some teams of sixth graders. To help group members feel more comfortable with this assignment, ask the teams to choose three questions to answer as they work on their own. Then when the teams report back, work as a group in answering each team's two unanswered questions.

Step 4
Help your sixth graders distinguish between the attitudes of Saul and David and focus more clearly on their own behavior. Before listing group members' responses concerning situations in which "insight" is needed, make two lists describing Saul and David. Title one list "Saul approach" and the other list "David approach." List such things as desire to please self (Saul), desire to please God (David), ruled by jealousy (Saul), and trusted in God (David). Then refer to these lists when you discuss each scenario.

Date Used:

Approx.
Time

Step 1: You're All Wet _____
o Large Group
o Fellowship & Worship
o Mostly Guys
o Extra Fun
o Short Meeting Time
Things needed:

Step 2: Asking for Directions _____
o Heard It All Before
o Mostly Girls
o Media
o Short Meeting Time
o Urban
Things needed:

Step 3: Word Perfect _____
o Extra Action
o Small Group
o Heard It All Before
o Little Bible Background
o Mostly Girls
o Extra Fun
o Urban
o Combined Junior High/High School
o Sixth Grade
Things needed:

Step 4: Saul or David? _____
o Extra Action
o Small Group
o Large Group
o Little Bible Background
o Fellowship & Worship
o Mostly Guys
o Media
o Combined Junior High/High School
o Sixth Grade
Things needed:

Honest to God

Choose one or more

☐ To help kids gain familiarity with the Old Testament wisdom literature, developing a basic biblical literacy.

☐ To help kids understand that God cares about our feelings and that we don't need to hide from Him.

☐ To help kids express their honest feelings to God.

☐ Other _____
_____

Your Bible Base:

Job 6:1-10
Psalms 42, 51, 73, 100
Proverbs 6:6-11
Ecclesiastes 1:1-14
Song of Songs 2:3-13

STEP

I

How Do You Feel?

O P T I O N S

Begin the session with a memory game. Have everyone sit in a circle on the floor. Start with one person who says, "How do I feel? I feel _____." The person should complete the sentence by naming an emotion and doing a simple gesture to represent that emotion.

For instance, the first person might say, "How do I feel? I feel *happy*." The second person then says, "How do I feel? I feel *happy* [acting out the first person's gesture], and I feel *angry*." (Of course the person may choose any emotion.) He or she must then come up with a simple gesture to represent his or her emotion. The third person then says, "How do I feel? I feel *happy* [acting out the first person's gesture], I feel *angry* [acting out the second person's gesture], and I feel *depressed* [acting out his or her own gesture].

Continue around the circle as far as you can, with each person repeating the words and gestures of all the previous people and adding one. Start over if you need to. You could make this a competition by having people drop out if they forget a word or gesture.

STEP

2

Denial? Me?

(Needed: Copies of Repro Resource 9)

Explain: **In this session, we'll be taking a break from the history of Israel and getting into its literature. There's a hunk of good reading in the center of our Bibles—Job, Psalms, Proverbs, Ecclesiastes, and Song of Songs.**

There are a lot of things we can learn from these books, but today we're going to focus on one in particular: God cares about how we honestly feel.

Refer back to the emotions named in the memory game. Ask: **If you** were feeling really happy about something, would you feel comfortable telling God about it? What if you were really angry about something—would you tell God about it? What if you were feeling jealous of someone? Get a few responses.

Some of your group members may not feel comfortable with talking to God about their "negative" emotions. If so, point out that if God wanted to hear only good things from us, He would have programmed us—like robots—so that we only experience positive emotions. (If applicable, you may want to refer back to your discussion from Session 1 here.) But since God cares about *every* feeling we experience, and because we often experience negative feelings, we should feel free to tell Him about those feelings.

Say something like: **God wants *real* people with *real* feelings. Unfortunately, some Christians haven't learned that yet. They're still pretending not to have negative feelings.**

Ask for four volunteers (preferably two girls and two guys) to perform a brief skit. Distribute copies of "The Stepford Christians" (Repro Resource 9) to the volunteers and give them a few minutes to read through the script. Then have them perform.

Afterward, discuss the skit, using the following questions:

Obviously, this was an exaggeration, but do you know people like this?

Does Christ really take away our feelings?

What does it mean to "rejoice in the Lord always"?

Is it possible to be joyful and still be honest about more "negative" feelings?

You don't need to answer all these questions right now. The Scripture study will help answer some. For now, you might merely say that Christ *does* change us. He turns a lot of negatives to positives. He does put joy in our hearts. But He never asks us to deny our honest emotions. He Himself wept and got angry. We are emotional beings, and God likes us that way.

STEP
3

Poetry in Motion

Ask: **When I mention the Psalms, what do you think of? What words come into your heads?** ("Praise," "joy," "The Lord is

HEARD IT ALL BEFORE

LITTLE BIBLE BACKGROUND

MOSTLY GIRLS

MOSTLY GUYS

SHORT MEETING TIME

JR. HIGH / HIGH SCHOOL COMBINED

SIXTH GRADE

my shepherd," "comfort," etc.)

I'm going to read a list of emotions and feelings. If you think an emotion is found in the Psalms, jump up out of your seat when I read it. If you think it's not found in the Psalms, kneel down in front of your seats. You *have* to vote one way or the other. Here's the list:

- **Anger**
- **Depression**
- **Loneliness**
- **Frustration**
- **Patriotism**
- **Nostalgia**
- **Fear**

Afterward, explain that *all* of these emotions and feelings are found in the Psalms.

Have group members turn to Psalm 42. Ask someone to read aloud verses 1-5. Then ask: **How is the psalmist feeling in this passage?** ("Downcast" and "disturbed.")

What do you think has happened to make him feel this way? (He knows that his hope rests in God, but God seems far away. People are challenging his faith, and he doesn't know what to say. He "used to" join the crowds at the temple, but apparently not anymore. Yet there is the hint that "I will yet praise him.")

Have you ever felt like this? If so, when? Get a few responses.

Have group members turn to Psalm 51. Ask someone to read aloud verses 1-12. Then ask: **How is the psalmist feeling in this passage?** (Ashamed, perhaps afraid of what God might do to him.)

What do you think has happened to make him feel this way? (He committed adultery with Bathsheba, and this is his prayer for forgiveness and cleansing.)

Have you ever felt like this? If so, when? Get a few responses.

Have group members turn to Psalm 73. Ask someone to read aloud verses 1-14. Then ask: **How is the psalmist feeling in this passage?** (Angry and/or frustrated.)

What do you think has happened to make him feel this way? (The wicked seem to be getting away with murder. The psalmist tries to be righteous, but it seems to be "in vain.")

Have you ever felt like this? If so, when? Get a few responses.

[NOTE: Don't leave this psalm without mentioning the conclusion in verses 16-19. As the psalmist renews his relationship with God, he becomes aware of the final destiny of the wicked. They may prosper temporarily, but ultimately God casts them down.]

Have group members turn to Psalm 100. Ask someone to read it aloud. (If you know music to this psalm, sing it together as a group.) Then ask: **How is the psalmist feeling in this passage?** (Glad, joyful, grateful, secure.)

What do you think has happened to make him feel this way? (Who knows? Maybe he just got an overwhelming sense of joy and security, knowing that we belong to a God who is so powerful, good, and faithful.)

Have you ever felt like this? If so, when? Get a few responses.

Bible Lit 101

(Needed: Copies of Repro Resource 10, pencils)

Explain: **There are four other books, in the same section of the Bible as Psalms, that we need to take a look at. This is sort of the "artsy" section of the Bible. And, just as artists are sometimes considered weird and unpredictable, these books are a little unpredictable too.**

Divide into four teams, and assign each team the following Scripture passages. If your group is small, divide into pairs or assign passages to individuals.

Team #1—Job 6:1-10
Team #2—Proverbs 6:6-11
Team #3—Ecclesiastes 1:1-14
Team #4—Song of Songs 2:3-13

Distribute copies of "Scripture Search #4" (Repro Resource 10) and pencils. Members of each team, after reading and discussing their assigned passage, should fill out the sheet together.

After 10-15 minutes, gather the teams together, and have each one report its findings. Use the following information to supplement the teams' responses.

Team #1
Assigned Text: Job 6:1-10
What title would you give this passage? ("What Am I Doing Here?" "Why?" "Hopeless," etc.)
Who is speaking? (Job, who has lost everything.)
Sum up in 15 words or less what is being said in this passage. (I wish God would just destroy me, before I curse him.)
What emotions are being expressed? (Sorrow, pain, frustration, depression, maybe anger.)
Do you think the person is right to feel this way, or doesn't it matter?

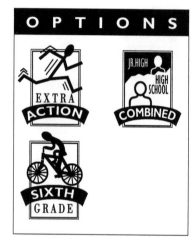

O P T I O N S

EXTRA ACTION

JR. HIGH / HIGH SCHOOL
COMBINED

SIXTH GRADE

(Yes. Job is honest about his feelings, but he wants to remain faithful to God. He realizes that God alone has the power over life and death. [This passage *sounds* suicidal, but Job would not have taken his own life—he left it in God's hands.])

Team #2
Assigned Text: Proverbs 6:6-11
What title would you give this passage? ("Ants Don't Cry 'Uncle!' " "Don't Be a Bum," etc.)
Who is speaking? (A wise teacher, probably Solomon.)
Sum up in 15 words or less what is being said in this passage. (If you are lazy, you will be poor.)
What emotions are being expressed? (Not many—perhaps just a stern warning.)
Do you think the person is right to feel this way, or doesn't it matter? (The author obviously feels strongly about the subject, and the advice he is giving is godly, so he does have a right to feel this way.)

Emphasize that many of the Proverbs are very practical in nature: "If you do this, this will happen." There's common sense here, even when there's not a huge spiritual lesson involved.

Team #3
Assigned Text: Ecclesiastes 1:1-14
What title would you give this passage? ("Meaningless," "Nothing New under the Sun," etc.)
Who is speaking? ("The Teacher" [Some say it's Solomon. Whether or not that's true, the book is written from a perspective of wealth, power, and leisure.])
Sum up in 15 words or less what is being said in this passage. (Everything repeats itself; it all seems meaningless. I've seen it all and it makes no sense.)
What emotions are being expressed? (Hopelessness, cynicism, depression.)
Do you think the person is right to feel this way, or doesn't it matter? (There's one thing missing here: a relationship with God. It is absolutely true that, *apart from God,* life has no meaning. So the Teacher is absolutely right in describing the emptiness of wealth, power, and pleasure.)

Team #4
Assigned Text: Song of Songs 2:3-13
What title would you give this passage? ("The Ultimate Love Song," "You Are So Beautiful," "Pass the Raisins," etc.)
Who is speaking? (A woman in love.)
Sum up in 15 words or less what is being said in this passage. (My lover is absolutely wonderful!)
What emotions are being expressed? (Love, passion, excitement.)

Do you think the person is right to feel this way, or doesn't it matter?
(Yes. Human love is a beautiful thing, and it's celebrated here.)

The Write Stuff

(Needed: Copies of Repro Resource 11, pencils)

Ask: **If these books were published today, how would they be marketed? In what sections of a bookstore would they be found?** (Job might be with the novels, or perhaps with the personal memoirs. Proverbs might be in the self-help section. Ecclesiastes might be in the philosophy section. And Song of Songs might be with the poetry or the gothic romances.)

Say: **We're going to try our hands at the types of writing found in these books. You may not think of yourself as an author, but that's OK. Just jot down what you feel—no one else will see what you write.**

Distribute copies of "Writing Styles" (Repro Resource 11) and pencils. As a group, briefly go over the instructions for the sheet and the examples given.

Then say: **Choose one of these styles and write a paragraph or so. This is just to get you started. Maybe you'll want to continue the exercise at home.**

Give group members several minutes to work. If anyone wants to share his or her writing with the group, you might allow that, but don't *force* anyone to share. These are meant to be personal communications with God.

Summarize: **Some people feel they have to pretend to be holy when they communicate with God. That's totally wrong. God wants us to come as we are. If we're confused, depressed, or lonely—He wants to hear it. If we're excited, in love, or just mellow—He wants to hear that too.**

Close the session with a group prayer, giving all of your group members an opportunity to say a sentence or two to God about how they're feeling.

THE STEPFORD CHRISTIANS

CAROL: (*To audience*) A bunch of my friends and I all became Christians around the same time. It was great. But then I noticed some strange things happening. It started with Becky.

BECKY: (*Entering, with a huge smile*) Hi, Carol!

CAROL: Hi, Beck. How are you?

BECKY: Wonderful! Couldn't be better!

CAROL: Good. How'd you do on that history test?

BECKY: I think I failed it.

CAROL: Failed it? Didn't you study?

BECKY: I tried. But I was reading about all those wars and everything, and it just seemed so negative. So I stopped.

CAROL: But doesn't that affect your final grade?

BECKY: (*Still smiling*) Yep. I may not graduate. Praise the Lord!

CAROL: Right. (*To audience*) And then I noticed the same sort of thing in my friend Jim.

JIM: (*Entering, with a huge smile*) Yo, Carol.

CAROL: Hey, Jim. Where's Joanne? (*To audience*) Those two are always together.

JIM: She broke up with me.

CAROL: Sorry to hear that. That must be tough to take.

JIM: Not really. All things work together for good, you know.

CAROL: But you really cared for her, didn't you?

JIM: Sure, but it's just as well. She got tired of my joyful attitude, I guess. She was really a pretty negative person, don't you think?

CAROL: No. Oops, I guess I'm being negative too. (*To audience*) Soon all my friends were smiling like that. There was something wrong with it all. And they all thought there was something wrong about me. One day a bunch of us were working at the church, putting some paneling in the youth room. Bob hit his thumb with a hammer.

(*BECKY and JIM are on stage, miming various work tasks. BOB mimes pounding a hammer, then hits his thumb.*)

BOB: Praise the Lord!

CAROL: Are you OK?

BOB: (*Smiling through clenched teeth*) In all situations, I have learned to be content.

CAROL: But you just hit your thumb with a hammer! You must be in pain!

BOB: I count it all joy to suffer for Christ's sake.

CAROL: No, Bob, that's wrong! When you smash your thumb, you say "Ouch!" not "Praise the Lord!" It's not natural.

BECKY: (*Advancing on Carol, zombie-like, still smiling*) But we don't live according to the sinful nature, Carol. We have a new nature.

CAROL: I know, but that's ridiculous!

JIM: (*Also advancing*) Do I sense anger in you, Carol? We've been praying that you would have a more joyful spirit.

CAROL: I do have a joyful spirit. But I have other emotions too. Can't a Christian have any honest feelings of sorrow or frustration, or even pain?

BOB: (*Advancing*) "Rejoice evermore," Carol. "Rejoice in the Lord always." Put away that negative spirit.

(*BECKY, JIM, and BOB advance until they're surrounding CAROL tightly. CAROL screams and hides her face. Then she looks up with that same eerie smile.*)

CAROL: (*To audience*) So now I realize how wrong all those emotions of mine were. We really should be happy all the time. Come on, guys.

(*ALL exit, singing, "I've got the joy, joy, joy, joy down in my heart."*)

Scripture Search 4

After reading your assigned passage(s) and introduction, answer the following questions as well as you can. You may have to do some extra thinking for some of the questions, because the answers may not be obvious in your text.

Team #1 Introduction: Job was a good man whose health and wealth were taken away by Satan (with permission from God). He remained faithful to God, though he had many questions about his suffering.

Team #2 Introduction: Proverbs is a collection of wise sayings giving practical and spiritual advice.

Team #3 Introduction: Many think Solomon wrote this "experimental essay," searching for the meaning of life.

Team #4 Introduction: This book is a love song in dialogue form. It celebrates the beauty of romantic love.

Assigned Text: _____

What title would you give this passage? _____

Who is speaking? _____

Sum up in 15 words or less what is being said in this passage. _____

What emotions are being expressed? _____

Do you think the person is right to feel this way, or doesn't it matter?

Writing Styles

Write your own biography-novel (like Job), psalm, collection of advice and common sense sayings (like Proverbs), experimental essay (like Ecclesiastes), or love song (like Song of Songs). Use the following examples to get you started. Choose one of them, and write your own piece of literature in the space below.

Biography-Novel

I was on my way to school one day, when suddenly I tripped over a branch that had fallen. *Why had God allowed that branch to fall in my path?* While I was puzzling over this, I tripped over a curb and sprained my ankle...

Psalm

YOU ARE GREAT, GOD! EVERY MOLECULE OF MY BODY SHOUTS YOUR PRAISE. EVERY SYNAPSE IN MY BRAIN, EVERY NERVE ENDING ECHOES THE CHORUS: GOD IS AWESOME!...

Collection of Advice and Common Sense Sayings

Maybe church is full of hypocrites, but can you think of a better place for them?
It is better to say one true word than a whole campaign speech.
When the going gets tough, it's just real tough, isn't it?...

Experimental Essay

I decided to figure out which kids at school really had the answers. So I went to the jocks and I asked, "Do you feel fulfillment and satisfaction?" And they said, "Uh, what's that?" . . .

Love Song

You are the pinnacle of God's creation. Your hair is woven by angels, your eyes the jewels of the heavens. I love being with you. I look forward to the times we spend together...

Step 4

Instead of having teams fill out Repro Resource 10, have them make up questions for a trivia game. Give each team five index cards. After reading its assigned passage, the team should make up five questions, writing the category and question on one side of the card and the answer on the other. One question should deal with the passage's *theme*; one should deal with the passage's main *character*; and one should deal with the *emotion* expressed in the passage. The other two questions can be about anything. When the teams are finished, collect and shuffle the cards. Choose one team to begin and ask the first question. If the team gets it right, award it the card and ask another question. If the team gets it wrong, move on to the next team; continue until one of the teams gets it right. The team with the most cards wins. After the game, discuss the different emotions and whether or not the people were right to feel that way.

Step 5

Have group members brainstorm a list of different emotions they face (and maybe situations in which they face them). List these emotions on the board. Then divide the kids into teams of three. Instruct each team to pick an emotion and make up a situation in which that emotion would be likely to occur. One of the kids on the team should play the "average teen," expressing the emotion and explaining the situation. Another should play a well-meaning adviser, giving the kind of false advice about feelings that some Christians give. The third should choose one of the writers or characters from the assigned passages (perhaps Job or the psalmist) and give biblical advice from that person's perspective. Each team will roleplay its situation for the rest of the group. Afterward, discuss the situations as a group, making further suggestions.

Step 1

Take advantage of the fact that your group is small by using the following activity in place of the "How do I feel?" game. Before the session, write several emotions on slips of paper. You might include anger, loneliness, frustration, happiness, etc. If you can't think of a different emotion for each member of your group, write some of the emotions on two slips. Put the slips in a bag. Begin the session by having kids pick a slip from the bag. Then have each person share a time he or she experienced that emotion. If kids say they've never experienced the emotions they picked, have them think of a time when they *might* experience them. This time of sharing not only introduces the theme of honesty but also helps your kids get to know one another better.

Step 2

Since you won't have a big audience, simply have your volunteers read "The Stepford Christians" skit (Repro Resource 9) from their seats, rather than making a big production of it.

Step 1

Make the memory game easier by breaking into two or three groups. Or try the following game as an alternative. Have your group members count off by fives and remember their numbers. Then instruct them to spread out all over the room. Assign one of the following emotions and its accompanying action to each number.
• sadness—cry "Boo hoo";
• happiness—laugh;
• anger—yell "Arrgh";
• fear—scream "Yikes! Help! Help!";
• depression—sigh loudly.
The object of the game is for group members to wander around making their sounds and listening to others until they gather all of their group. (You can make it a contest if you want to.)

Step 5

Instead of having individuals work on "Writing Styles" (Repro Resource 11), have teams write progressive poems. Divide the kids into teams of four. Give each team a pencil and a sheet of paper. Instruct the teams to fold the paper accordion-style, so that there are eight sections. One person on each team will write the first line of a poem about feelings. However, no one else on the team may see what he or she writes. This person will then hand the sheet to the next person, telling the person only the last word of the line. The next person must add a line, making sure that the last word rhymes with the last word of the previous line. Continue until the first stanza is done. To begin the next stanza, start the process over again with a different rhyming word. When everyone is finished, have volunteers from each team read the poems.

Step 3

Jaded kids may "turn off" when you turn to the Bible. So, before considering how the Bible addresses a variety of emotions and the problems which cause them, give your group members a challenge. Have them come up with situations that they think will "stump" the Bible. Have group members write these situations on slips of paper; then collect the slips and compile a list. After you go through the list, point out that you'll be reading Scripture passages by people who were almost suicidal, madly in love, hopelessly cynical, and full of financial advice. After studying the Bible passages, refer back to the list to see how these passages (or others) address the feelings and problems the kids raised.

Step 5

One way to overcome cynicism is to help kids see that the Bible addresses the problems *they* face. Have group members form teams of three. Each team should write a "Dear Christian" letter in which an imaginary character describes his or her problem. (If you used the "Heard It All Before" option for Step 3, encourage group members to refer to that list for ideas.) When the teams are finished, have them read their letters aloud. Then have the rest of the teams suggest what "Christian" might write in response. You could vary this idea by having teams exchange their "Dear Christian" letters and write replies to each other. You could then share the letters and replies with the rest of the group.

Step 2

Kids who are unfamiliar with Christianity and the Bible will probably not be able to generalize about some Christians. They also might not be familiar with the pressure to be positive that some Christians place on each other. Consequently, you'll need to modify this step. First, to determine your kids' understanding, ask: **How do you think Christians are supposed to feel?** Then either explain the skit a little more—it exaggerates the misunderstanding of some Christians—or skip it if you think it might confuse non-Christians or young Christians. Finally, you'll need to modify the discussion of the skit. Unchurched kids won't know what Christ teaches about feelings. Instead, explain His teaching and give kids an opportunity to ask questions.

Step 3

The beginning of this step probably won't work well for kids with little Bible knowledge, since they'll probably draw a blank at the mention of the word "psalms." Explain that Psalms is a book of 150 "songs." Point out that many of the psalms were written by David, the Israelite king, but that there were many other writers too. The psalms were collected over the years. In a way, the book is like a hymnal without the music. Having provided this background information, you might ask kids what kinds of emotions they think would be expressed in a book of religious songs. Discuss why they feel that way.

Step 1

Use this self-disclosure game before or in place of the memory game. Distribute a pencil and a slip of paper to each group member. Instruct group members to think about themselves—their likes, dislikes, interests, personality, strengths, weaknesses. Then have them think of the Bible character or famous Christian (living or dead) that they think they're most like. Have them write the name of that person on their paper along with a sentence or two explaining why. Finally, go around the room and have volunteers share their responses. You might start the sharing yourself. (If you have a large group, you might break into teams of five for the sharing time.) When everyone is finished, spend a minute or two discussing why it's sometimes difficult to be honest about ourselves.

Step 5

Instead of having group members work on "Writing Styles" (Repro Resource 11), prepare a multimedia worship time. Begin by having group members brainstorm a list of the emotions that kids their age most often feel. Then divide group members into different teams according the medium they want to work in: words, music, or art. (If you have a lot of kids who choose one particular medium, divide it into smaller groups.) Have each team create something directed toward God that expresses something that kids often feel. Writers could write prayers or poems; musicians could practice to perform an appropriate song; artists could make murals or collages. (You will need to have art supplies and possibly some instruments available.) Close the session by having group members present their creations to each other and to God.

Step 2

Instead of a two-guy-two-girl skit, change "The Stepford Christians" (Repro Resource 9) slightly and do it twice. Ask two teams of four volunteers each to perform the skit. Have one team perform it as if all the characters were girls. Use the same dialogue, but change Bob's name to Roberta, change Jim's name to Jamie, and have Jamie talk about her boyfriend. Have the other team perform the skit as if the characters were all guys. Change the names of Carol and Becky to Carl and Ricky. After both teams have presented the skit, talk about our attitudes about how people "should" or "should not" show emotion.

Step 3

After reading and discussing David's emotions as described in the Psalms, talk about displaying emotions in public and in private. Say: **The Psalms were a personal expression of David's feelings. Would it have been inappropriate for him to express those feelings in public? Why or why not? Do you think everyone, male and female, has emotions similar to those described by David? Under what circumstances do most people show emotion in public? What is the difference between hiding your emotions and not displaying them in public?**

Step 1

Many guys will be uncomfortable with the memory game since it puts them on the spot and makes them act out emotions. Instead, try the following variation. Get group members playing a game like basketball, volleyball, or floor hockey. Explain that periodically you will blow the whistle and shout an emotion. When you do, group members will have to stop playing and act out that emotion. They will probably find acting out emotions together less threatening than acting them out individually.

Step 3

Guys often have difficulty expressing emotions. In large part, this is due to the fact that our society discourages such expression—it's not "manly." One result is that guys can have difficulty being honest with God and themselves about their feelings. This session provides a good opportunity to talk about this difficulty and to explore biblical examples that counter our society's influence. Ask your group members why they think guys have difficulty expressing emotions. Ask volunteers to share about times when they expressed emotions and talk about how people responded. Point out that the psalmist is male and that he was not ashamed to express his emotions to God. Encourage group members to seek this same kind of openness and honesty.

Step 1

Clear out an area of the room and have your group members stand in a circle in that area. Ask for a volunteer to join you in the center in the circle. Give this person a tossable object (balloon, beanbag, large coin, etc.). Explain that you will name a sound. When the person throws the object in the air, everyone in the circle must make the sound and then must stop the precise moment the object hits the ground. The last person to stop will come to the center and be the next tosser. Keep playing unitl everyone but one person is in the center. Be sure to use sounds that are related to emotions. For example, you might have group members laugh, cry, yell angrily, sigh despondently, etc.

Step 5

After the session, let group members decorate sugar cookies with faces that express different emotions. You will need one to three cookies per group member, frosting (probably of different colors), plastic knives, paper plates, napkins, and plastic baggies. (You can put frosting in a baggie, cut the corner, and squeeze the frosting out for decorating.) Ask volunteers to bake the cookies and bring frosting. After kids have made their cookies, have them show the cookies off and guess the emotions being expressed before eating them. You might even have a contest to find the saddest cookie, the happiest, etc.

Step 2

Have group members evaluate the kinds of messages that can be found in contemporary Christian music. Bring in tapes of several songs (or portions of songs) or ask your group members to bring some of their favorites. Play the songs for your group members, asking them to concentrate on what the lyrics say about the feelings that Christians have or should have. After you've listened to four or five selections, have group members rate the songs on a scale of 1 to 10 according to honesty (with 10 being the most honest). After group members rate each song, ask: **How often do you feel this way? How realistic is this song in showing how most Christians really feel? What does the Bible say about this feeling?**

Step 5

Explain to your group members that the Bible passages in this session present the feelings and views of a person in pain, a cynic, a lover, and a wise man. Point out that popular culture also presents us with a variety of feelings and viewpoints. Have group members listen to some popular songs and compare the feelings and views they express to those of the Bible. Try to find songs that touch on subjects like suicide, the meaning of life, advice for living, and love. Listen to the lyrics of the songs and then compare them with the Bible passages. How are they similar? How are they different? (If you have trouble finding contemporary examples, ask a couple of your group members to offer some suggestions. You might also use older songs for the activity, like "Suicide Is Painless" [the M.A.S.H. theme song], "Love Stinks" by J. Geils Band, or "Bang on the Drum All Day" by Todd Rundgren.)

Step 1

If you're short on time, you may want to skip the memory game in Step 1. You could begin the session with the explanation in Step 2 concerning the Books of Job, Psalms, Proverbs, Ecclesiates, and Song of Songs.

Step 3

Don't read and discuss all of the psalms as a group. Instead, assign the psalms to smaller groups to read and report on. Or, if you need to save even more time, choose one psalm to read and discuss as a group, and give the references to the other psalms. If you do the latter, you might want to read Psalm 47, in which the psalmist is "downcast" and "disturbed." This psalm is especially helpful in countering the pressure that many Christians feel to always be happy and cheerful and to deny their own negative feelings.

Step 1

If your group members are like most urban teens, they may refuse to sit on the floor. This is due to the fact that many urban young people tend to take an almost "religious" pride in their clothing. Therefore, to sit on the floor is to "defile" and to sacrilegiously make "unclean" their garments of sacred holiness. (OK, maybe it's not that extreme.) But if your group members are pretty serious about their clothes, have them play the game while seated in chairs instead of on the floor.

Step 5

As group members work on Repro Resource 11, you might want to include some literary options urban teens may be more familiar with. Offer the following suggestions:
Street Language Prose
Yo, baby, I'm down wit' Jesus because He's God and my number one homeboy. So since Jesus is clockin' us all, you better step-off and get Him. 'Cause wit' God you'll be the def'est homeslice this side of that chumpie called Beantown.
Rap Prose
Some call him God.
Some call him Jesus.
But all I know,
He cannot leave us.
Back in the day
When I was lost,
Jesus died upon the cross.
So if you don't want hell
To be your home,
Call him up
On your prayer phone.
For only this God can be this good.
Jesus—number one in the neighborhood.

Step 3

Although we all experience similar emotions, high schoolers will probably be better at articulating emotions than junior highers will. Ask several volunteer high schoolers to participate in a panel discussion of emotions. Explain that each participant on the panel will be representing an emotion (loneliness, depression, patriotism, fear, anger, frustration, nostalgia, etc.). Instruct each panelist to prepare a brief presentation of his or her assigned emotion. He or she may define the emotion, talk about how it feels, talk about how it affects the way you look at others and at God; and/or give a personal example of a time he or she experienced the emotion. After the presentations, let the rest of the group members ask questions if they wish.

Step 4

As you divide into teams, you might compose Team #4 of high school students, since they will be studying the Song of Songs. Where junior highers might be embarrassed discussing romantic love, high schoolers may find it especially applicable to their dating lives.

Step 3

Help your sixth graders more easily identify the emotions described in the Psalms by reading shorter portions of Psalms 51 and 73. For example, after discussing Psalm 42:1-5, read Psalm 51:1-4 and talk about David's shame before God. Then read Psalm 51:10-12 and discuss it. Read Psalm 73:1-3 and 12-14, and talk about the emotions described in each portion of Scripture.

Step 4

Sections of "Scripture Search #4" (Repro Resource 10) may be difficult for some teams of sixth graders. To help group members feel more comfortable with this assignment, ask the teams to choose three questions to answer as they work on their own. Then when the teams report back, work as a group in answering each team's two unanswered questions.

Date Used:

Approx.
Time

Step 1: How Do You Feel? _____
o Small Group
o Large Group
o Fellowship & Worship
o Mostly Guys
o Extra Fun
o Short Meeting Time
o Urban
Things needed:

Step 2: Denial? Me? _____
o Small Group
o Little Bible Background
o Mostly Girls
o Media
Things needed:

Step 3: Poetry in Motion _____
o Heard It All Before
o Little Bible Background
o Mostly Girls
o Mostly Guys
o Short Meeting Time
o Combined Junior High/High School
o Sixth Grade
Things needed:

Step 4: Bible Lit 101 _____
o Extra Action
o Combined Junior High/High School
o Sixth Grade
Things needed:

Step 5: The Write Stuff _____
o Extra Action
o Large Group
o Heard It All Before
o Fellowship & Worship
o Extra Fun
o Media
o Urban
Things needed:

Fun and Prophet

YOUR GOALS FOR THIS SESSION:

Choose one or more

☐ To help kids gain familiarity with the Old Testament prophets, developing a basic biblical literacy.

☐ To help kids understand major prophetic themes—justice, trust, the coming kingdom, and the suffering servant.

☐ To help kids trust God in their daily lives and act more justly toward others.

☐ Other _____

_____

Your Bible Base:

Isaiah 52:13—53:9
Amos 5:11-17, 21-24;
    6:4-7
Hosea 11:1-5; 14:1-4
Zechariah 8:3-8, 14-17

First Names First

(Needed: Prizes)

Begin the session with a quiz. Divide into two teams. Those group members whose first names begin with the letters A-J will be one team; those whose first names begin with the letters K-Z will be the other team. Announce that the team that answers the most questions correctly will win a prize (perhaps candy bars or some other edible treat).

Seat the A-J team as close to you as possible; seat the K-Z team farther away. As you give the quiz, consistently favor the A-J team. Try to be subtle about it at first. For instance, if an A-J team member is close on an answer, give him or her the point. If a K-Z team member is close, don't award the point. A team gets one point for each correct answer.

The first four questions are general questions. The first person to raise his or her hand gets to answer. However, when you can't tell who raised his or her hand first, give the benefit of the doubt to an A-J team member.

1. Name the four Beatles. (John Lennon, Paul McCartney, George Harrison, Ringo Starr) A-J team members may give just the first names; K-Z team members must give first *and* last names.

2. What book of the Bible comes after the Book of Numbers? (Deuteronomy.) If a K-Z team member answers first, make him or her spell the word.

3. In the 1992 winter Olympics, who won the gold medal for women's figure skating? (Kristi Yamaguchi.) If a K-Z team member answers first, make him or her spell Kristi's last name.

4. When was the War of 1812 fought? (1812-1815.) Accept "1812" from an A-J team member; but insist on the entire time span from a K-Z team member.

The next four questions are "grab bag" questions. The first person to shout out the correct answer wins. But as you read the questions, try to speak very softly, so only the A-J team members (who are closest to you) can hear. In a close call, "hear" only the A-J answer.

5. What is the capital of [your state]**?**
6. Who was Columbus, Ohio, named after?
7. What sport is Eric Lindros known for? (Hockey.)
8. What TV show features Homer, Marge, and Bart? (*The Simpsons.*)

The final six questions are "back-and-forth" questions. Each team will have an opportunity to answer three questions without having to race against the other team.

9. For the A-J team: **Where was Jesus born?** (Bethlehem, stable, manger—accept any reasonable answer.)

10. For the K-Z team: **Who was governor of Syria when Jesus was born?** (Quirinius.)

11. For the A-J team: **How many corners does a triangle have?** (Three.)

12. For the K-Z team: **How do you determine the area of a right triangle?** (Side A times side B, divided by two.)

After the first twelve questions, if the A-J team is somehow losing, award enough points on these final two questions for the A-J team to win.

13. For the A-J team: **What is your favorite color?** (Accept anything.)

14. For the K-Z team: **What is the capital of Burkina Faso?** (Formerly known as Upper Volta, this African nation has as its capital Ouagadougou. [Good luck pronouncing it.]) In case some whiz kid answers it correctly, ask for a spelling, or the earlier name of the country, or what *Burkina Faso* means—"land of upright men."

Tally up the points and award the prize to the A-J team. Then talk about the activity.

Ask the K-Z team members how they felt during the quiz. Chances are, they were upset, at least at first. Some may have been challenged to beat the setup; others may have just given up.

Explain: **Contests aren't fun when they're not fair—at least for the team being treated unfairly. The A-J team probably had a good time. But there was injustice done during this contest.**

Discuss *how* you showed favoritism during the quiz. Group members might mention your speaking softly on some questions, your "selective hearing" of responses, the difficulty of certain questions, or the differences in how specific the answers needed to be.

Then ask: **What injustices or unfairness do you see in our society today?** Encourage several group members to respond to this question. Have them consider many different areas of society. For instance, would they say society's "system" is tilted against certain races? Against women? Against teenagers? Against children? Against the poor? What examples can they give?

Explain: **Today we're going to talk about some men who were very concerned about injustice—the Old Testament prophets. These men often served as the "conscience" of ancient Israel, making sure that things were done right and that people were treated fairly.**

STEP
2

All the News That Fits

(Needed: Copies of Repro Resource 12)

O P T I O N S

When I say the word "prophet" or "prophecy," what do you think of? (Predictions, seeing the future, "psychic connections," end-of-the-world visions, etc.)

Explain: **The fact is, Old Testament prophets were more concerned about the events of their day than they were with the future. They were more like news commentators than psychics. From time to time they needed to give perspective by referring to some future event—and God allowed them to see some future events—but these were always related to some present-day need of the people. The prophets weren't only foretellers, they were forthtellers, speaking forth the nitty-gritty truth of God in tough times.**

Maybe a skit will give us a better idea of what these prophets were like.

Ask for five volunteers (preferably four guys and one girl) to perform the skit. Give each of them a copy of "Prophecy Network News" (Repro Resource 12). Let the actors read through the script once to familiarize themselves with it; then have them perform.

Afterward, ask: **From what you saw and heard in this skit, how would you describe the job of an Old Testament prophet?** (Reminding the people of Israel what God's will was for them and warning them of the consequences of not following His will.)

STEP
3

Four Finds

(Needed: Copies of Repro Resource 13, pencils)

Explain: **After Solomon's kingdom split in two, both the northern kingdom and the southern kingdom had prob-**

lems—both international and spiritual. As we saw in the skit, the prophets kept warning that God would judge His people unless they turned away from their false gods and trusted Him for their strength.

As the "news report" showed us, the Assyrians conquered the northern kingdom in 722 B.C., and took away those tribes. Those Israelites who were taken away settled in other areas, where they intermingled with the locals and lost their national identity. That's why some people call them the "ten lost tribes" of Israel.

Assyria very nearly conquered the southern kingdom as well; but the faithfulness of King Hezekiah helped to fend off disaster for a while. Around 600 B.C., the next great empire, Babylon, came sweeping through the region. The prophet Jeremiah kept warning that the Jews would be defeated, but no one listened. There were several invasions, and finally, in 586 B.C., the Babylonians destroyed the temple and carried off many of the Jews.

For seventy years, the Jews waited in Babylon. The prophet Ezekiel, in his strange ways, kept assuring the people that God was not finished with them yet. In one vision, he saw a valley full of dry bones that were coming to life again. Sure enough, the Jews got permission to return home, and many did. Leaders like Ezra and Nehemiah led the attempts to rebuild Jerusalem—and the temple. Prophets like Haggai, Zechariah, and Malachi tried to motivate the people.

Let's take a closer look at some of these prophets and their prophecies.

Divide into four teams, and assign each team the following Scripture passages. If your group is small, divide into pairs or assign passages to individuals.

Team #1—Amos 5:11-17, 21-24; 6:4-7
Team #2—Hosea 11:1-5; 14:1-4
Team #3—Isaiah 52:13–53:9
Team #4—Zechariah 8:3-8, 14-17

Distribute copies of "Scripture Search #5" (Repro Resource 13) and pencils. Members of each team, after reading and discussing their assigned passage, should fill out the sheet together.

After 10-15 minutes, gather the teams together, and have each one report its findings. Use the following information to supplement the teams' responses.

Team #1
Assigned Text: Amos 5:11-17, 21-24; 6:4-7
How would you describe the feelings behind these verses? (Anger, disappointment.)

Do these verses deal more with the future or the prophet's current situation? (Mostly current, with a hint of future judgment.)

What situation(s) does this passage describe or predict? (Rich people were cheating and oppressing the poor, and "playing at" religion without it affecting their behavior.)

Which theme most closely fits this passage? (The need to act with justice toward others.)

How do you think the hearers of this passage responded? (Some may have changed their ways, but many probably laughed it off as the rantings of a crazy prophet. The people felt pretty secure in their phony religion.)

How could these verses make a difference in the life of a young person in today's society? (He or she might treat poorer or less "cool" classmates with honor.)

Team #2

Assigned Text: Hosea 11:1-5; 14:1-4

How would you describe the feelings behind these verses? (Deep disappointment, unrequited love.)

Do these verses deal more with the future or the prophet's current situation? (Mostly current, with a promise of future love and a hint of judgment.)

What situation(s) does this passage describe or predict? (Israel had been turning to other gods and persisted in doing so. Judgment had to come, but God longed for Israel to turn to Him.)

Which theme most closely fits this passage? (The importance of trusting God.)

How do you think the hearers of this passage responded? (Some may have renewed their relationship with God and forsaken their idols. Others may not have paid attention.)

How could these verses make a difference in the life of a young person in today's society? (He or she might consider the "false gods" that he or she is tempted to turn to—money, popularity, sex appeal, drugs, etc. The person might also choose to trust God, rather than "false gods," for his or her success and satisfaction.)

Team #3

Assigned Text: Isaiah 52:13–53:9

How would you describe the feelings behind these verses? (There is sorrow for the suffering, but an underlying appreciation for the salvation it brings.)

Do these verses deal more with the future or the prophet's current situation? (It deals with the future, in terms of a suffering Messiah. But it might also be referring secondarily to the current [at that time] sufferings of the Jews.)

What situation(s) does this passage describe or predict? (A servant of

God who would bear the sins of all people, taking punishment upon Himself.)

Which theme most closely fits this passage? (The vision of a suffering Servant-Messiah.)

How do you think the hearers of this passage responded? (The people probably identified with this text, since they had suffered too. It might have given meaning to the pain they'd felt, understanding that God Himself suffers, and that suffering leads to redemption.)

How could these verses make a difference in the life of a young person in today's society? (He or she might rely on Christ as the payment for his or her sins, and accept forgiveness from God. He or she might be more willing to suffer, if necessary, to stand up for Christ.)

Team #4
Assigned Text: Zechariah 8:3-8, 14-17
How would you describe the feelings behind these verses? (Joy, determination.)

Do these verses deal more with the future or the prophet's current situation? (Future, with implications for present behavior.)

What situation(s) does this passage describe or predict? (God promises to establish a safe and prosperous kingdom, but He requires true and just behavior.)

Which theme most closely fits this passage? (The promise of God's coming kingdom.)

How do you think the hearers of this passage responded? (With joy, gratitude, and a determination to please the Lord by rebuilding a righteous society.)

How could these verses make a difference in the life of a young person in today's society? (They might give him or her something to look forward to or challenge him or her to live righteously. They assure him or her that no matter how bad life is now, there is a better world coming.)

STEP
4

Making a Difference

(Needed: Chalkboard and chalk or newsprint and markers, copies of Repro Resource 13, pencils)

Ask: **What about you, as a young person in today's society? What do the themes listed on the resource sheet mean to**

you? How can they change your life?

Write the following on the board: "The Importance of Trusting God." Say: **We saw how the leaders of Israel and Judah often trusted in their international alliances rather than in God. And the people of Israel often worshiped other gods.**

What things do people put their trust in today? (Money, insurance, social position, job security, sex appeal, relationships, their own abilities, etc.)

How can you show your trust in God? (Obeying Him in certain situations; pulling out of bad relationships; making God-centered decisions about everyday issues; forgetting about your own status with your group of friends, and doing what's right.)

Write group members' responses on the board as they are named. Then write "The Need to Act Justly toward Others."

Say: **We saw how the prophets, especially Amos, scolded the people for their lack of justice. They thought they were very "religious," while they ignored the needs of the poor around them.**

Refer to the items group members named earlier as examples of injustice in our society today: the rich getting richer while the poor get poorer; laws that favor the rich; the special treatment received by "beautiful" or famous people; racism and sexism; etc.

Ask: **What can you do to act more justly? And is there any way you can change the "system" of our society?** Group members may have ideas about political activity, such as letter-writing campaigns and so forth. But also steer them toward justice in their personal lives. What kids do they hang out with? Do they show favoritism toward beautiful or wealthy people? If so, what can they do to change that?

Again, write group members' responses on the board. Then write "The Promise of God's Coming Kingdom" and "The Vision of a Suffering Servant-Messiah."

Say: **We saw how Zechariah and Isaiah gave different visions of the future. One spoke of a wonderful, peaceful kingdom. The other spoke of the suffering of a righteous Messiah.**

How do these truths affect what you do? How can they change your attitudes and actions? (There is encouragement for tough times in both truths. There should be appreciation for Christ's sacrifice, and a new perspective gained by the vision of the future kingdom.)

Write group members' responses on the board as they are named. Then ask group members to choose *one* thing they can do in the next week to (1) show their trust in God, (2) act more justly toward others, or (3) show their appreciation for God's coming kingdom or the suffering Servant.

Have group members write their ideas on the back of Repro Resource 13—as specifically as possible. Announce that you're going to check on their progress at your next meeting.

Close the session in prayer, asking God for strength and determination for your group members as they attempt to carry out theirs. Thank Him for the suffering of His Son and for His future kingdom.

Prophecy Network News

ANCHOR: Good evening, everyone, welcome to Prophecy Network News. Top stories this century include the dismantling of Solomon's empire, and the growth of false religion in the north. We turn to our man on the scene, Elijah.

ELIJAH: Thanks, Christine. I'm here on Mount Carmel, where the prophets of the false god Baal are going through their antics, trying to get a response from their god. It's no use, guys! Chill out, will ya?

ANCHOR: Some of our viewers may wonder how things got to this point. It seems that Ahab, the king of Israel, now actually *supports* Baal-worship.

ELIJAH: Oh, yeah. Ahab's into that whole scene—he and his wife Jezebel. When David was king, he was great. Then came his son Solomon, and Solomon was even greater—for a while. Toward the end there he started drifting away from God. When Solomon died, the country split up. The southern kingdom stayed loyal to Solomon's son, but the northern kingdom followed one of Solomon's assistants and set up a new dynasty. The southern kingdom has had a lot of problems, but at least they have the Temple. The northern kingdom set up its own worship centers and things went downhill from there.

ANCHOR: So what's happening there now?

ELIJAH: Well, I challenged the Baal-worshipers to a duel, sort of. We both offer sacrifices, and if they can get their god to send fire from heaven to consume the sacrifice, they win. But they've been at it all day. Baal must be on vacation, or in the john or something.

ANCHOR: What about your sacrifice?

ELIJAH: I'm getting that ready now, pouring water on it, just to make it interesting. OK, I think it's time. (*Praying*) Lord, show them all who's God. Accept this sacrifice. (*He mimes the onrush of fire.*) Whoa! Did you see that? The fire came down—it was amazing! You saw it here, folks, live from Mount Carmel. Back to you, Christine.

ANCHOR: We're now in the 700's B.C. Let's turn to our southern correspondent, Isaiah. How's everything in Jerusalem?

ISAIAH: King Ahaz is going to ruin this nation with his military policy. I've told him so, and he will not believe it.

ANCHOR: Just so our viewers know, this is Ahaz, king of Judah in the south, not Ahab, who used to be in the north.

ISAIAH: Yes, Ahaz is a descendant of King David, so he has no excuses. But he's not showing anything close to the kind of trust David showed.

ANCHOR: What do you mean?

ISAIAH: Everyone's worried about Assyria and their big war machine. I mean, they're just rolling right through the Middle East. No one can defeat them—except God, of course. But Ahaz is conducting a border war with two smaller nations. He's actually worried that these two pipsqueak nations will defeat him, when he should be concerned about Assyria.

ANCHOR: And he should be trusting God, right?

ISAIAH: Exactly. Now it looks like he's going to make a treaty with the huge Assyrian army to get them to take care of these tiny nations. It's like hiring a hit man to settle a playground fistfight.

ANCHOR: Is there any hope, Isaiah?

ISAIAH: In the future, yes. God will send a Prince to lead His people. He will be a Wonderful Conselor, the Mighty God, the Prince of Peace. We don't know when that will happen, but we're all looking forward to it.

ANCHOR: Let's go to the northern kingdom, with Hosea standing by. Sorry to hear about your family crisis, Hosea.

HOSEA: Thanks, Chris. Normally I don't like to talk about my personal life on the air, but this illustrates what's happening in Israel right now. My wife has left me, just like Israel has left the Lord. I've done everything I could for her. I send her gifts and flowers, but she thinks these are coming from her other lovers. In the same way, God has provided for Israel, but the Israelites are now thanking Baal for these gifts. I'm really afraid that some pretty nasty judgment is on its way.

ANCHOR: Thanks, Hosea. Now we have a lifestyle report from Amos.

AMOS: It makes me sick, Christine. The rich are getting richer, and they're just crushing the poor people. I'm here in Jerusalem and I see all these society women making a big show of going to the Temple. The jewelry, the fancy clothes—they spend all day lounging around and eating while the rest of us have to work for a living. I saw one of these women literally step on a beggar by the Temple gate. Honestly, it's like a herd of cows trampling the poor. If that's the way they practice their religion, it's worthless. It makes me sick.

ANCHOR: Thanks, Amos. There are some late-breaking developments in the northern kingdom. We understand Assyria has overrun Israel and is deporting its people. Let's see if we can get a report. Hosea? Hosea? The lines seem to be down. Isaiah, in Jerusalem, what can you tell us?

ISAIAH: Well, Hosea was right when he predicted judgment for the north. It seems that God is using the Assyrians, as wicked as they are, to execute His judgment on His people. I'm worried that the southern kingdom, Judah, may face the same problem if we don't shape up.

ANCHOR: But you have a new king in there, right?

ISAIAH: Yes, it's Hezekiah, son of Ahaz. This fellow looks promising. He seems to trust God in every situation—and we certainly have a situation here. I just received word that an Assyrian army is surrounding Jerusalem. It looks pretty bleak. But—get this—King Hezekiah has declared a day of prayer. He himself is asking God what to do. This is the kind of trust we've needed for a long time.

ANCHOR: That's good to hear, Isaiah. We'll stay with that story as it develops. Still no word from the northern tribes. We seem to have lost touch with them… What's that? Back to Isaiah for an update.

ISAIAH: There's been a miracle here, Christine. Some scouts have returned from the Assyrian camp. There are hundreds of Assyrian soldiers dead, and we don't know how it happened. It's as if an angel from God struck them down, in answer to Hezekiah's prayer. The mood here is joyous, almost giddy, as those reports are confirmed. Jerusalem has been saved.

ANCHOR: Thanks. That's all we have time for this segment. For Elijah, Isaiah, Hosea, and Amos— thanks for joining us. See you next century.

Scripture Search 5

After reading your assigned passages, answer the following questions as well as you can. You may have to do some extra thinking for some of the questions, because the answers may not be obvious in your text.

Assigned Text: _____

How would you describe the feelings behind these verses? _____

Do these verses deal more with the *future* or the prophet's *current* situation? _____

What situation(s) does this passage describe or predict? _____

Which of the following themes most closely fits this passage? (Circle one.)
- The importance of trusting God
- The need to act with justice toward others
- The promise of God's coming kingdom
- The vision of a suffering Servant-Messiah

Consider the situations of those who received these prophecies.
- Amos—The southern kingdom was riddled with corruption.
- Hosea—The northern kingdom was turning to Baal-worship.
- Isaiah—The Jewish community was being held hostage in Babylon.
- Zechariah—The Jews were back in their homeland, after their Babylonian captivity, trying to pick up the pieces.

How do you think the hearers of this passage responded? _____

How could these verses make a difference in the life of a young person in today's society? _____

Step 3

Before group members work on Repro Resource 13, have them play a quick game. Before the session, you'll need to write down several Old Testament events that you've taken from a timeline (perhaps in the back of a study Bible). Put each event on a separate slip of paper. Shuffle the slips and have group members work together in putting the events in proper chronological order.

Step 4

Have group members brainstorm a list of injustices that exist in their immediate worlds (family, school, sports, clubs, neighborhood, church, etc.). List the suggestions on the board as they are named. Then have group members form teams of three. Instruct each team to choose one injustice from the list to act out for the other teams. The other teams will then try to guess what it is. Afterward, discuss ways that kids could act more justly in these unjust situations.

Step 1

Instead of using the quiz, give group members an opportunity to share personal experiences. Instruct group members to sit in a circle. One at a time, have each person complete this statement: "One unjust or unfair thing that happened to me was …" After everyone has completed the first statement, have each person complete this statement: "One unjust or unfair thing that I did was …" If group members seem hesitant to respond, get them started by sharing your own experiences first.

Step 4

If your group is small, you have a real opportunity to develop a sense of community and caring. A good way to do this is to have group members share personal needs and pray for one another. After group members have written out their plans for trusting God and acting more justly, have them form pairs. Instruct the members of each pair to share their plans and pray for each other. An alternative would be to have all of your group members share their plans with each other and then close the session with a time of group prayer. If you choose the latter option, you may still want to pair up group members and have the partners commit themselves to calling each other during the week for progress reports and encouragement.

Step 1

As an alternative to the quiz, play "Jail." Have group members form two teams. Instruct the teams to face each other. Team members will throw balls at the opposing team. If they hit a person, that person "goes to jail" (stands behind the opposing team's line). A person in jail can get out if his or her teammates throw a ball over the opponents and he or she catches it. The team that gets all of its opponents in jail wins. To introduce the idea of injustice, give one team an advantage over the other. For example, you might allow the favored team to free several prisoners at a time, instead of one. Or you might free its prisoners for no reason. Or you might not force its players to go to jail when they are hit with a ball. Follow up the game with a discussion of fairness and justice.

Step 3

Use the following idea as a way for teams to study their passages and share them with each other. After each team has read its passage(s) and completed the worksheet, have it make a display that explains its passages. Give each team poster board and markers. Explain that the teams must create something that will help the other teams quickly understand their passages. If they need help getting started, suggest that they pick out key words or verses and use illustrations or diagrams. When the teams are finished, allow them to circulate, reading the worksheets and looking at each other's displays.

HEARD IT ALL BEFORE

Step 2
Since kids who've heard it all before probably know the Old Testament pretty well, they might not appreciate the overview in the "Prophecy Network News" skit. Instead, it might be more helpful to have them spend time exploring problems in our world before they turn to the Bible. Have group members work in teams of three or four. The members of each team should consider three things about the world (society, school, church, home, etc.) that make them angry, that they find unfair or unjust. Distribute poster board and markers to the teams and have them make murals depicting the three things they came up with. After the teams have shared their posters, explain that the Bible prophets also got mad about things in the world around them.

Step 4
Help group members apply biblical principles to contemporary problems by becoming "prophets." Encourage group members to follow the model of the Old Testament prophets in creating a prophecy for today. They should point out a problem in society, explain God's view (His displeasure or a principle being violated), and give a call to repentance and change. Allow group members to work individually or in groups and in any medium you have available. You will need to supply things like pencils, paper, markers, drawing paper, and clay. Wrap up the session by allowing group members to proclaim their prophecies. Perhaps you could even display these prophecies for the rest of the church.

LITTLE BIBLE BACKGROUND

Step 3
Help group members understand the passages better by providing some of the following background information: Amos was a farmer-turned-prophet. In his day, most people in Israel were optimistic about their country and the future. Hosea, whose name means "salvation," was also a prophet to the northern kingdom, shortly after Amos. Isaiah was a prophet to Judah. He was well-educated and spent most of his time in Jerusalem. His book has been called a miniature Bible: the first thirty-nine chapters (like the thirty-nine books of the Old Testament) declare judgment on human sin, and the last twenty-seven chapters (like the twenty-seven books of the New Testament) proclaim a message of hope. Zechariah was appointed by God to encourage the people as they were rebuilding the temple. Zechariah's name fits his book; it means "Yahweh (the Lord) remembers" or "Yahweh has remembered." It means that God has remembered His covenant with His people.

Step 4
Help your group members increase their Bible knowledge by developing a sense of Bible history and the prophets' place in it. Have the teams from Step 3 work on timelines of the kingdoms of Judah and Israel and especially of the prophets. Provide poster board, markers, and resources like study Bibles with charts and Bible encyclopedias. The timelines should include key events, reigns of kings, and periods of various prophets. The teams may also illustrate their timelines, particularly the entries for the prophets they studied in the session.

FELLOWSHIP & WORSHIP

Step 1
Depending on how much time you have, use the following activity in addition to or in place of the quiz. Have group members form a circle. Then ask each person to complete the following statement: "If I were president, three things I would change are ..." If your group is large, have kids line up alphabetically by middle names; then divide them into teams of four. Have the team members share their completed sentences with each other.

Step 4
Distribute hymnals to your group members. Instruct them to find hymns that correspond to the topics of the three discussion questions: trusting God, acting justly, and accepting God's promises. If possible, have them try to find at least one hymn for each topic. (For instance, "Standing on the Promises" could correspond to the topic of accepting God's promises.) Then sing the hymns as a group to close the session.

Step 2

Ask for five volunteers to read the "Prophecy Network News" skit (Repro Resource 12). Ask the four girls who are to represent the four prophets to reword the information as if they were the press secretary or public relations agent for that prophet. Have the girls read through the skit to familiarize themselves with it and plan how to appropriately represent what their prophet would say to the public.

Step 3

As the four teams are reporting their findings from "Scripture Search #5" (Repro Resource 13), have them ask for discussion from the entire group on the last question. However, they should reword the question as follows: "How could these verses make a difference in the life of a young woman in today's society?" Ask group members to name differences for their personal lives and then differences for those they know who are in economic or cultural situations different from theirs.

Step 1

Instead of using the quiz, get guys thinking about issues of justice by playing a sport unfairly. If you have the space and equipment, play a game of volleyball. As referee, you should gradually start calling the game lopsidedly, letting one team get away with anything, while calling a tight game (a lot of lifts, double hits, throws, etc.) for the other team. For the favored team, you can "miss" certain infractions by claiming you didn't see them. A simpler option would be to have a free-throw contest (or toss a beanbag at a trash can). Allow one team to move closer or get a second try. You might even count near misses. After playing the game (and probably hearing a lot of complaints), discuss what made the game unfair.

Step 4

Focus your discussion of injustice on issues that guys may find especially pertinent. Encourage them to explore the following issues of justice and fairness:
- **For those of you who play sports, do you think it's unfair that some people get a lot of playing time while others get very little?**
- **When you're playing a pick-up basketball game, are there unfair ways to choose up sides?**
- **Have you ever been unfairly accused of being sexist? If so, how did you feel? If not, what would you do if you were?**
- **What are some unfair or unjust things that guys do because they're guys?** [NOTE: Obviously this could involve dating issues, but it could also involve other issues as well.]

Step 1

Instead of using the quiz, play a "hot-air relay game." Have group members form two teams. Give each person a straw. Each team will get a piece of tissue paper that members must pass to each other. They should do so by sucking through their straws so that the tissue is held against the straw. If they drop the tissue, they can't use their hands, but must use the straw to suction it from the ground. The first team to pass its tissue down the line wins. To introduce the idea of injustice, give one team a piece of tissue and the other team a paper towel. The tissue should be much easier to manage, giving that team an unfair advantage. Play the relay game and then discuss issues of fairness.

Step 4

After the discussion, end the session with a "prophet relay." You will need two boxes, each with a robe, a "prophet's hat" (any kind of hat), and a "prophet's belt" (a piece of rope). Have group members form two teams. The first person on each team will run to the box, put on the prophet's clothes, shout "Turn from evil and obey God," take off the prophet's clothes, and run back to the team. The next person will then run to the box and do the same thing. Repeat the process until all the players have finished. The first team done wins.

Step 1

Rather than discuss different kinds of injustice, have group members find examples in magazines and newspapers. Bring in a stack of magazines and newspapers. Have group members (individually or in teams) cut out as many examples of injustice as they can find. Give them a few minutes to work; then have them share their findings. You might also have group members make a collage out of the articles, especially headlines and photographs. You can refer to these clippings later in the session.

Step 4

Have group members brainstorm a list of the kinds of injustices that exist in their daily lives. Then have them come up with ways they could act more justly in these situations. Next, divide them into teams. Have each team create a public service message targeted at junior high students. The message should challenge kids to act justly in areas where they often don't. Examples might include things like "Don't make fun of other kids" or "Don't exclude certain kinds of kids from your cafeteria table." If possible, you might want to tape the messages on video or audio cassettes. Then you could have the teams play their messages for each other.

Step 1

Instead of using the quiz, distribute candy in an unfair manner. Bring in a bag of hard candy or small candy bars. Have group members line up to receive the candy. However, you should only give the candy to certain people. Perhaps you might give it only to people with blonde hair and blue eyes. Or you could have group members hold out their hands and give the candy only to people holding out their left hand. Afterward, discuss the fairness of your distribution system as a way of introducing the topic of justice. Then distribute candy to those group members who didn't receive any.

Step 2

Skip the "Prophecy Network News" skit (Repro Resource 12) and instead concentrate on the definition of prophets. This discussion will prepare your group members for studying the prophecies in Step 3.

Step 1

Here are some additional questions you might want to include in the opening quiz:
1. Name any three Michael Jackson albums produced since 1978. (*Dangerous, Bad, Thriller, Off the Wall.*)
2. How many Native-Americans were there in Congress in 1993? (One.)
3. Who is the host of "Soul Train"? (Don Corneilius.)
4. What is M. C. Hammer's real name? (Stan Burrell.)

Step 3

After the teams have completed Repro Resource 13, ask: **What do you believe is the overall purpose of a prophet of God?** After a few minutes of discussion, give the following definition: "A prophet is one whom God uses to proclaim the truth in spite of the consequences." With this definition in mind, ask group members to consider who the prophets are in their city and community. List the names of these people on the board, as well as the characteristics that qualify them as "prophets." Then present these "prophets" as role models for your group members to emulate.

Step 1
After you finish the quiz, get group members thinking about injustices in society, especially their own surroundings, by having them draw pictures of common situations in their schools. They could do this individually or in teams. Encourage them to depict a "typical" sixth, seventh, and eighth grader or a "typical" freshman, sophomore, junior, and senior. Encourage high school and junior high kids to compare their pictures. You might concentrate especially on the way eighth graders are "top dogs" in junior high, but "low men on the totem pole" as freshmen. Discuss the fairness of each situation, focusing especially on the way the students are treated and the way they treat others.

Step 4
During this discussion period, you might find it helpful to divide into groups according to age. This may be especially true as kids consider ways in which they can act more justly. Encourage kids to think about their daily situations, rather than big social problems. Since the situations of junior highers and high schoolers are quite different, splitting them up should facilitate discussion and practical application.

Step 3
Since the biblical content is very abstract, limit the Bible study to the passages in Amos and Hosea (Team #1 and Team #2). Have group members form two teams. Instruct the teams to choose three questions to answer as they work on their own. Then when the teams report back, work as a group in answering each team's two unanswered questions.

Step 4
Do only part of this step. Write the following topics on the board and discuss each one: "The Importance of Trusting God" and "The Need to Act Justly toward Others." Then have group members choose one thing to do this week concerning one of these topics and write it on the back of Repro Resource 13.

Date Used:

Approx. Time

Step 1: First Names First _____
o Small Group
o Large Group
o Fellowship & Worship
o Mostly Guys
o Extra Fun
o Media
o Short Meeting Time
o Urban
o Combined Junior High/High School
Things needed:

Step 2: All the News That Fits _____
o Heard It All Before
o Mostly Girls
o Short Meeting Time
Things needed:

Step 3: Four Finds _____
o Extra Action
o Large Group
o Little Bible Background
o Mostly Girls
o Urban
o Sixth Grade
Things needed:

Step 4: Making a Difference _____
o Extra Action
o Small Group
o Heard It All Before
o Little Bible Background
o Fellowship & Worship
o Mostly Guys
o Extra Fun
o Media
o Combined Junior High/High School
o Sixth Grade
Things needed: